The Column I Never Wrote

John Masterson

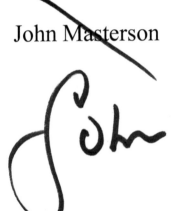

The Harvest Press

The Column I Never Wrote

By John Masterson

Published in 2022

by The Harvest Press

www.theharvestpress.ie

ISBN 978-1-8380836-4-9

OUT OF BODY

"It's not your child."

I was nineteen. My pregnant seventeen-year-old wife of five days was lying beside me in my childhood home. My parents were asleep across the hall.

I do not have great trust in memory. Over the years I have written about false memories I have discovered myself having. I wrote about the time my father closed the car door accidentally on my hand. I can still see my finger hanging off and the bone exposed. I have the scar to prove it. The visual memory is as strong as it was that sunny afternoon in Dunmore East beside our blue Austin A40.

It never happened. What did happen was my father almost shut the door on me, thinking I was already in the car. He stopped in time. I wasn't even bruised and an ice cream cone got rid of any frightened tears. The scar came from some later minor childhood accident I don't even recall. The image in my memory probably began being formed with some childish exaggeration in school the next day and, having gained some attention, it grew and grew. It always surprises me how easy it is to modify the truth. And then believe it.

This is not something that only happens in childhood. As recently as 2020 I fell down the stairs of an eight foot high deck outside my house while moving a heavy table. I hit the ground hard and broke several bones. I didn't move for about ten minutes, though I was conscious, and just getting my bearings, and figuring out how to get help and wondering would I be able to walk to the end of my lane. Some three weeks later, after a spell in hospital and an operation, I told the story on local radio of how I had summoned help. I had realised I had a phone in my pocket and an Apple Watch on my wrist and had used one or other to ask Siri to phone for help. I marvelled at how useful technology had become and wondered how long I would have lain on the ground otherwise. It was a good story and I told it well. I was just telling it as I remembered it. Clear as day, and again, it didn't happen quite like that.

It was some months later before a friend told me what had actually happened. By pure coincidence, she had phoned me when I was lying on the ground. I answered and asked her to get in the car and come and get me. She arrived about twenty minutes later and took me to hospital. I have no idea where the made-up story came from. I certainly did not intend to lie, or think I was lying at the time. There is a postscript to this story and I tell it because it is a good illustration of how stupidly one can behave under stress. People who wear an Apple Watch will tell you that one of its irritating features is if there is any sharp movement it will ask you if you fell. Try chopping a log with the watch on and after one connection with the wood the watch will be talking to you. You answer that you did not fall. Then it asks are you ok, and you reply you are. Then you take it off and put it in your pocket! On the day I had my fall, the watch did its usual check immediately. "Did you fall?" Despite the fact I had just flown through the air, I told it I had not fallen. When it asked me was I ok, I replied 'yes'. I had broken my collarbone and four ribs and punctured a lung but somehow I couldn't admit this to Siri. Pride also comes after a fall.

Whatever about my distrust of memory, I am clear about that teenage night, lying in that bed, hearing it's not your child spoken quietly, in fear and trepidation, and about several other events around that time. I do believe most of my recall is at least close to the truth. I have not spoken about it often so there has not been a lot of opportunity for alteration or embellishment. Barry Gibb, not far behind Paul McCartney in songwriting success, has said that there are things that he cannot talk about. But he can put them in a song. This book is my song.

My girlfriend had not been able to have sex since I had returned from a J1 working summer in America a few weeks earlier, unaware I was facing into a rapid and unplanned marriage. There was always some excuse.

Now married, just a few weeks later, her body still wouldn't allow her. There were no more excuses. She seemed physically unable to allow me to enter her. This was certainly odd for newly-weds. We had been through a lot and I did not make an issue of it. On the fifth night she told me the truth. I have often thought about those few words in the intervening fifty years. I feel a mélange of emotions as I think of them now. 'It's not your child' will stop you in your tracks, even if it's not in the same league as 'I'm sorry, it's terminal cancer' or watching a judge don a black cap and telling you that you are going to be hanged by the neck until you die. But it is up there.

3

I can still see the bed, the room, the patterned pink and blue wallpaper, and all from above as I look down, as if from the ceiling, on the young lost couple, each lying in the bed, staring blankly upwards without the remotest idea what to do. I am on the left and she is on the right. It is the one and only time in my life that I had an out of body experience. I had never even heard of the phenomenon. There was absolute silence until, eventually, I was able to speak. I thought of my parents sleeping nearby and in hearing range, were either of us to raise our voice. I didn't look at her. I looked at the cheesy wallpaper. The pattern is fresh in my mind.

We can't tell anyone. We have caused enough upset, was all I said. She didn't disagree. I cannot remember if I asked who the father was. I know she did not tell me. I am not sure if she knew for certain, though she did know it was not me, and had known when she had written to me in Washington DC on one of those tissue thin prepaid aerogrammes we all filled with tiny writing to save money. She had known when I rang her from a street coin box for a rare prearranged call, when she waited at my parents' house. Not everyone had a phone back then. She had known when I landed some weeks later in Dublin Airport at 8.15 on Thursday 26 August, where she was waiting with my parents. She had seen me off in May and they were kind enough to ask her if she wanted to come to the airport. Little did they know. I had not even bothered changing my flight, because I knew what she was telling me was impossible.

Sometime later one of her friends gave me a name. Later, another friend named the brother of that person. I still do not know the truth, nor does it matter to me in the least. The night before I went to America we shared a bed and, while there was affectionate intimacy, pregnancy would have been about as likely as the Immaculate Conception.

I cannot remember if I lay awake that night she told me the truth or went into a deep sleep. We must have got up and had breakfast the next morning and carried on as if nothing had happened. I probably played golf because that is what I did at every opportunity. My diary of those days, which I still have, is fairly blank. It says my Senior Freshman exams began on 22 September and third year lectures began on the 18th October. I didn't enter anything on the wedding day. The next entry was playing golf on the Trinity team against Lahinch in December. I lost my match.

I don't think of that night, or those times, every day. But almost half a century later I do still think of them often. I always listen with interest when I hear people who were subjected to the abusive treatment that was the norm in Mother and Baby homes and some schools. There is anger and pent up emotion. Their hurt still seems very raw despite the passage of time. Their wounds appear much more open than my one that opened that night when I learned of the deception I had been walked through. Many years later I did spend troubled months when everything surfaced again. The events became as real again as if they had happened the previous week. They dominated my every waking moment, and my sleep became a torture. If I slept. I became very angry with the world when I was made aware of people who had watched me walk down that aisle in the full knowledge I was being suckered. The person who told me this was equally angry. She was a well grown-up married woman by then. On the day I became a husband she was beside me, an unborn, unexpected and definitely unplanned child, who began life the following February. A baby we named Áine. There were two innocent parties at that altar.

I know that out of body night changed the course of my life for ever. It must have influenced many decisions and much of my behaviour throughout my life. There are people who know me who tell me I have never ever dealt with it. I don't know what dealt with it means. I cannot forget it. I am still very aware of those, and subsequent days. I am not sure time always heals. Sometimes it just applies a bandage and stems the flow for the time being.

I have wondered whether therapy would make me feel more aware, more at ease, happier, less troubled. I doubt it. Would therapy lessen the effect it has on my decisions, emotions and ability/inability to deal with closeness, my lifelong want it desperately followed by can't cope with it pattern? Again I doubt it. It is probably too late to go to the mental repair shop and get some reprogramming, though people I know well have all but begged me to do something. Will writing it down help? Maybe.

I am not one for sitting in a comfortable chair, in a book-lined office, revealing my innermost secrets and attempting to achieve greater self-understanding. It seems a little self-indulgent given that, while I may be a very flawed person, I am a fully functioning member of society. Perhaps I just haven't been found out. Like many people, I am, at times, curious to know more about how I became the person I am, and wonder if things could have been different. I know I am capable of saying I have no regrets one day, and listing hundreds of regrets within the following week. Or even day. My psychological scars may have damaged me, but not crippled me, so I am content to live with them. No one lives a trouble-free life and I had a big bang early. I want to understand myself, but not necessarily change the bits of me that make up the person I feel I am. There are, no doubt, wounds that have not healed, but I prefer to look at them for what they are rather than talk them into insignificance. Shit happened.

I often wonder at how practical I was in the weeks before and after those four words. I seemed to be on automatic pilot. I had been in the USA for 3 months on a J1 visa working in an ice factory (yes, a factory which did nothing but make ice) on the midnight through to morning shift the locals would not do. There were six of us, all Irish students. We shared a two-roomed basic flat with mattresses on the floor. We lived like monks. We had girlfriends at home and were ridiculously faithful. We saved hard. There was no kitchen and we lived off a one plate electric cooker where we alternated between scrambled egg and rice with soup for three months, and daily self-service lunches in Scholl's café down the street which probably kept us alive.

I was studying Philosophy and Psychology in TCD and we never had a typical summer as our exams took place in September for some unknown reason. Along with one of my classmates I spent a lot of my days buried in books or arguing about psychology. Apart from that, the summer was about making money and not spending it. The six of us lived opposite the hotel where years later John Hinckley shot and almost killed Ronald Reagan. Our building was over a greengrocery shop and the owner offered us the first week free if we painted the place. We did. He got a good deal. He had said hello to two of us when we were buying an apple and asked if we were from Ireland. Our Aer Lingus shoulder bags were a good clue. We were fairly naive travellers. Ten minutes later we were his tenants. Lee lived on the ground floor with his lover, Ed. It was the first time any of us had experienced a perfectly normal gay married couple living together openly and happily. Weekends were busy and we met lots of friendly people on the stairs. Midway through summer we came across our address in an underground free newspaper. Our top floor was the venue for weekend gay parties and film nights. Sadly we were six heterosexual males. We could have had a great time without even going out our front door.

Daytime we did touristy things. I loved the Smithsonian and was mesmerised to go into the Space Museum and see things like the Lunar Module up close. We walked around the historic areas of Washington DC, spent afternoons sitting at the reflecting pool, looked at the White House and saw a helicopter take off one day. It had to be Marine 1. We convinced ourselves Nixon was inside. We went to concerts if they were free. I remember seeing Spencer Davis playing acoustic at P Street Beach.

The J1 system was, and probably still is, a godsend to Irish students. I went to America three years running and would return home in August with plenty of dollars. Then, just when things were getting tight, a tax rebate would arrive in January. I had bought a pair of very trendy (or so I thought) patched jeans to bring my girlfriend as a present. They would make her stand out even more from the crowd! I think she hated them. When it comes to presents it's the thought that counts is never true.

The Column I Never Wrote

I am not mean but I am better at buying for myself. Most of us bought
Frye cowboy boots while in the US, wore them on the plane home because
they were hard to pack, and lived in them for the next few years. The first
summer several of us bought good cameras we could not afford in Ireland.
Once home the next essential was a stereo system, followed by a new
supply of LPs. The remaining few hundred dollars were for living.

Towards the end of my summer in DC my girlfriend told me she
thought she was pregnant. Today I am not certain if the news arrived in
an aerogramme, or via a very rare phone call. I know I told her on a later
call that it was impossible, to stop worrying, and I thought little more
about it.

I accompanied her to the doctor a few days after my arrival back in
Ireland. My diary says it was at 12.30 on Tuesday 31st, the Tuesday after
I returned home. I was fully confident this concern was silly and feeling
a bit embarrassed as the doctor knew my family and was the same person
who had seen me through childhood measles and mumps. I sat outside
while the examination took place. In what seemed like a very short time
I was sitting there with the doctor telling us together what she had already
told my girlfriend in the privacy of her consulting room, that she was three
months pregnant.

I have never passed that building, no longer a surgery, without
remembering walking down those steps that lunchtime. We probably
went for coffee in Kyteler's Inn and stared across a table at each other. Or
maybe we walked down by the river and clung on to each other as if there
was no tomorrow. Looking back I had limited understanding of the fear

9

and panic, the desperation a teenage schoolgirl from a Catholic family felt on knowing for certain she was facing into provincial Ireland's greatest shame. She was going to be an unmarried mother and there was nothing whatsoever that could change that fate. She was going to be looked at on the street, gossiped about, listen to mock pity and pious crap and be told forever that she ruined her life.

We decided to tell no one until we had worked out what to do. Abortion was not really an option back then. It was barely spoken of. We wouldn't have had an idea of how to organise it, though oddly we could have afforded the trip across the water with my American money and money she was making from singing. She was a talented young woman who worked hard and played hard, harder than I thought at the time. She told me she had already drunk a bottle of gin in as hot a bath as she could stand but to no avail. That was as far as termination went for young Irish girls back in the 1970s.

1971 was a time of rapid change through the world. The summer of love had already gone sour. Peace and love were becoming sex and drugs. The Beatles were no more. John Lennon released *Imagine*, and moved to New York, never to return. The Monkees had already been and gone. Mick Jagger married Bianca and the Stones released *Brown Sugar* which sounds as fresh today as it did fifty years ago. Jim Morrison died. Lee Trevino won the British Open. John Newcombe and Evonne Goolagong won at Wimbledon and Kilkenny didn't win the All Ireland. Alan Shepard became the fifth man to walk on the moon. We got decimal currency. Margaret Thatcher ended free school milk for children over seven and was forever Thatcher the Milk Snatcher. Internment without trial was introduced in Northern Ireland. Charles Manson got the death penalty but it was never carried out. Irish television's viewers had a diet of *The Riordans*, *Seven Days* and *Wanderly Wagon*. Condoms could not be bought in Ireland. Women had to quit their jobs when they married. It was a full quarter century before divorce would be legalised. And, I find it hard to believe, 1971 was the year women got the vote in Switzerland.

That my girlfriend had conceived about two weeks after I left the country made perfect biological sense. But she assured me nothing of the sort had happened and so I chose to accept that the well-nigh impossible was the only feasible alternative. Why, I often wonder? I suspect because a first teenage love can be very strong and stupidly blind. But also because I had grown up in an environment where being truthful was highly valued. I recall my father often defining a lie as the intention to deceive. That is a very high bar. I think I simply was unable to believe someone could lie to my face about something so important and with such huge consequences. It was easier to accept the impossible.

That left me with no alternative but to do the honourable thing. I have no recollection of telling my parents that my girlfriend was pregnant and we were getting married. That was something no parent wanted to hear. My parents would, I suspect, have been more concerned about the long term effects on my life than on the short term scandal. They made it clear that, from their point of view, they did not expect us to get married. And, in fairness to her, my girlfriend also told me it was not necessary. She did not pressurise me. There was no hard sell. I felt marriage was what I had to do and walked headlong into the trap. Plans were put in place and we were wed a few weeks later in Dublin.

I sometimes wonder was there a bit of the rebel in me on that day. Was I thinking it was that bit cool to be married and soon to be a father at nineteen? I do remember making the Ringo Starr "Peace and Love" V sign coming out of the church and being told by a family friend that it didn't look good. I still cringe when I think about it. I am not sure if I am remembering an event or a photo of the event. As to the day, I know of no photos that still exist. I suspect my mother burnt everything. But, more surprisingly, I have no memory whatsoever of the ceremony or small reception that followed in a Dublin hotel. I just cannot conjure up the tiniest recollection. Did I make a speech? I have no idea. Did my father make one? Again I don't know. Were any of my friends there? I can only recall my somewhat non-plussed best man, a friend from schooldays. Thus began my five days of marriage. I do remember the small hotel we stayed in for one night, the first of the nights when lovemaking did not happen. There is something psychologically odd about not being able to recall more than one or two seconds of one's wedding day.

I must have said I do. When the congregation was asked if there was anyone who knew of an impediment, or any reason why this marriage should not take place, there was silence. I always go back to my father's definition of lying, the intention to deceive. You can do that without opening your mouth.

PUPPY LOVE

In boarding school it was very cool to get letters from a girlfriend. I was fortunate to be in a co-educational school and I still believe all education should be co-ed. I know of no good reason for keeping the sexes apart for six formative years. I am still in contact with some of the girls with whom I was in class. There were lots of teenage crushes that did not amount to much. To have a girlfriend outside the school had some added frisson. When the post came, envelopes were laid out on the hall table for all to see. I remember the excitement of seeing her handwriting. And the fear that I would soon be reading I had been dumped. She was far from the most prolific correspondent, but I never got a Dear John. In those teenage years I would read and re-read her words, looking for all sorts of nuances that weren't there.

I don't remember exactly when we met. We would have been parts of intersecting groups of teenagers that roamed the town and eyed each other up. She would always have been on my radar in the holidays when I was home from Dublin, if I was not on the golf course which was where I spent most of my time. There were lots of attractive teenage girls but, from when I first saw her, she was the one I wanted. Plenty of other young males in the town would have shared that ambition. I probably met her properly the summer before my Leaving Cert when I was about sixteen and she was a very mature fourteen. I am sure she was a great deal more worldly wise than I was. She had some great stock phrases. I can still hear her saying, you deserve a leather medal if I ever said anything she heard as the tiniest bit boastful.

Teenagers went to the Carlton ballroom on a Saturday night and the target was to have a girl by the time Fleetwood Mac's *Albatross* was played and to walk her home. With luck you would have some sort of snog on the way, or even at the gate of her house. I recall a priest getting on stage one night and taking the microphone to instruct the young males that he didn't want to see any of us mollicking the young girls. It is not a word I have heard before or since, but it had something to do with close slow dancing and he felt perfectly entitled to disrupt proceedings.

I didn't have a car or access to one. The strongest drink on sale in the Carlton was Club Orange, though we may have visited a pub first. Raiding the parents' drinks cabinet was not a runner because there wasn't a lot in it … maybe a bottle of gin and one of whiskey and some sticky liqueur that had seemed like a good idea in Spain and hadn't been touched since. They would have noticed.

I was proud of my pinstripe jeans and flowing red satin shirt with ruffled cuffs. There must have been girls who left the building before the slow set for fear of being approached by this apparition who thought he was in The Small Faces. Young males were drenched in Brut after-shave, despite barely needing to shave. We tried to be trendy and psychedelic, a word we had read in the *New Musical Express* but weren't sure how to pronounce. I saw an early Thin Lizzy, or more likely it was Skid Row, playing in The Carlton. Phil Lynott appeared to be learning the bass guitar on stage that night. We danced, and didn't really listen, which seems like heresy now. I can still hear the local boys, The 5th Degree, begin with *Paint it Black*, a Stone's cover.

The soundtrack of teenage years usually stays with us through life. I remember the excitement of the Doors and *Light My Fire*, the extraordinary new sounds that Pink Floyd made. I practically wore out The Incredible String Band's *The 5,000 Spirits or the Layers of the Onion*. Leonard Cohen's *Songs from a Room* with *Suzanne* and *Hey, That's No Way to Say Goodbye* would have been on repeat if we could do repeat. I climbed over the wall in boarding school one Sunday and went down to Dolphin Discs to get *Sgt Pepper*. We just could not believe what we were hearing and even today I am aghast at the creativity of that album. They were exciting times. Our gang had no time for showbands. They were at the other end of town in the Mayfair, for old people in their twenties or people who came in from the country.

Neil Young's *After the Gold Rush* was an album I played a lot around that time. I usually shared a house in Dublin with a few friends when I was a student. We probably hadn't much more than a dozen LPs each so they were all well played. I can never hear the words "Lover, there will be another one, who'll hover over you beneath the sun" without being catapulted back into those days. I sometimes remember her by the river on a sunny day, making love in our youthful fumbling manner on the rare occasions when I had been able to find a condom to buy from a student down from Northern Ireland. But when I hear that song the lover I imagine, to this day, is some anonymous figure. It wasn't me. I was

15

working in a factory in Washington DC, making two dollars fifty an hour and taking all the overtime on offer, while she was at home living life to the full. Deferred gratification was not her strong suit.

It seems hard to believe today that smuggled condoms from Northern Ireland, or the infamous rhythm method, were the only protection against pregnancy if you had abandoned abstinence, as many of us had. It was a nice earner for Northern students in TCD, despite the fact that we were already paupers compared to them with their huge government grants. We didn't have cars. Some of them had sports cars. We were so innocent that it was not unheard of for the prospective purchaser to be asked what size they would like – small, medium or large. It was also said that condoms were so scarce that they could be washed out and used again. I am not entirely sure this did not actually happen. As to sensitivity, I can remember paying for a rubber that had all of the quality of a washing up glove.

By teenage fidelity standards, which mostly referred to snogging, or heavy petting which was the very dated term in vogue, she got around. In that regard she was probably not a lot different from most young people, including me, or her school friends. We were a bit young for going steady and relationships were on and off every few weeks. Excitement and experimentation were in the air. Carnaby Street set the colour code. Skirts were short and school uniforms were taken off once outside the school gates. Way out was the new norm. The Beatles and the Rolling Stones had blown away a lot of cobwebs. She was not one to turn down opportunities. I am sure someone had made a pass at her before I landed in the USA. There would have been no shortage of rivals delighted that I was off the stage.

Going out together meant we went to the cinema where it was normal to kiss for the full ninety minutes after the lights went down and barely know what film was showing. We sometimes walked by the river. We must have done a lot of talking. I always walked her home and there is a building I still see where we eked out the last few minutes kissing, winter and summer, before her time to be home had arrived.

She played guitar and sang well. She and her sister were winning talent competitions around the South East and being paid by local pubs to turn up at weekends and play in the corner. They would sing *Scarborough Fair* with the two sisters' voices blending and people would listen … two guitars, two voices that harmonised instinctively, singing songs like *Blowin' in the Wind*. It was the era of the singing pub, an abomination that stalked the land for a few years when, unfortunately, many beautiful old pubs were modernised. There had to be some entertainment because apparently no one would enjoy a quiet pint and a chat. Some of the music was awful but these two sisters were good and had a following. I still hear stories about some of the continentals who had been attracted to Kilkenny by the Design Workshops going to great lengths to save some of the city's beautiful old pubs as landlords felt they had to get in on the craze. It will pass, they were persuaded, and indeed it did. But while it was there the sisters were in demand and it provided very good cash for two teenagers.

She was beautiful, funny, talented and full of mischief. I have very few photos of her but she had features that would be attractive in any generation. She always stood out in a room and would not look out of place in a magazine today. In those distant pre-politically correct days the phrase was fine thing. She definitely was one. Sadly she bit her nails. I can still see them on the fretboard.

She was already a well-hooked smoker in her teens and it was something we fought about. I hated smoking even then but didn't have a lot of success dissuading her. She had me wrapped around her little finger.

I was rebellious and cheeky, and a bit gawky with acne covered in Clearasil, the way teenage boys could be. I tried to grow my hair long but it only seemed to grow wide. The instant I left school I grew a beard and probably looked a little bit too much like Charles Manson. To my surprise she liked me. I was that bit older, but two years is a lot at that age. I was in a Protestant boarding school in Dublin, which was that bit different, and known to be clever. I lived near the golf course and was playing off a 4 handicap which is healthy enough and later got me on the Trinity team for a while. I wish I could play remotely like it today. The golf course was a world foreign to her though we all met up on Saturday nights when the club ran fundraising dances open to all. Sometimes there was a group, again local heroes, The 5th Degree.

I always suspected I was punching above my weight, but despite the fact that I have had relationships with fabulous women through my life, I still retain those doubts. I can't blame her for that. The surprise is that I ever put anyone on such a pedestal again.

Many of the teenagers in Kilkenny fancied her rotten and she knew it. She could flirt. Older guys with cars were attracted to her, and back then a car was the ultimate status symbol and better than a bedroom in terms of the privacy it offered. She knew she was considered very good looking but she wasn't too hung up on it. I don't think she would have been obsessed with selfies had they existed. I varied between being immensely proud to be by her side, and madly jealous if anyone, particularly someone with a car, asked her out. She would tell me nothing ever happened. Did it? Possibly, but I have no idea. She could pretty much pick and choose. I remember her telling me, in a state of great confusion, that a youngish priest had told her he would leave the priesthood if she would marry him. She was still a schoolgirl at the time. What did I do to bring this on? she wondered.

She drank a bit too much for her age, but I don't ever recall her actually being drunk. The binge drinking of today hadn't really been invented. We couldn't afford it. She had more spending money than most teenagers and was probably helped along by an alcohol gene, if there is one, inherited from her father. It was a curse that most likely influenced some of the poor decisions she made in her short life.

I loved her with the fierceness that only an adolescent can. There are times in life when one thinks about someone night and day, but I don't think they ever compare with that teenage obsession which is a combination of novelty, hormones, self-doubt and unstable self-esteem.

Today my memories of her are fond, affectionate ones. Her photo pops up occasionally on my laptop and I smile. I think of how her life and mine could have been so different. Would we have stayed together if the pregnancy had not happened? I doubt it. We were at the age when the vast majority of young romances bite the dust. I was already focused on Dublin, psychology and the rest of the world. There is a small chance that I would have left her first. I tried in my first year in college. Always the drama queen, she threatened to kill herself. That was, of course, nonsense. What is doable today was scarcely thinkable back then. But it shook me. It was enough for me to go to the college psychiatrist with a cock and bull story and get some pills that made me feel great and decide not to move on at what would have been the ideal time. She would have got over me by the next weekend.

Would we have remained friends? I would like to think so.

My life collided with hers, disastrously for both of us. Perhaps we had no choice but to live it. That was our destiny. People sometimes fall in love with the wrong people, or perhaps the right person at the wrong time. With a few different bounces of the ball things might have been different. My mother liked her, even after it had become clear Áine was not my child, and we had parted. She often said to me, in her more generous moments, that it would not have been impossible for us to work it out. No one forced us to get married. There was no shotgun, rather the reverse. We were advised to wait. We just felt, or perhaps I just felt, it was what we had to do, or should do. But no one really tried to stop us either. Crucially no one raised the issue that would have blown it all apart. There were people who knew the truth and they chose to keep their mouths shut. I walked down the aisle wearing a stage suit borrowed from a guitarist friend. Whenever I wonder what the woman beside me thought I always remind myself she was a very young girl in a bad situation in a moralistic judgemental gossipy country. If I resent people for not telling me the truth then she is not one of those.

There is a song that always reminds me of those days. If it comes up on my iPod I sit down and listen. It is called *I Could have Told You*, written by Jimmy van Heusen & Carl Sigman and made famous by Frank Sinatra. The singer is really talking to himself and trying to make sense of a failed romance, and bemoaning those who could have told him that it was all so predictable, that she would love, leave and hurt him.

Bob Dylan, a lover of the Great American Songbook, recorded it more recently and I love the plaintiveness of his version as he does his best to find the notes, singing about sleepless nights and her making promises that won't be kept as she moves on. Bob sings through the tears about all who could have told him so. But would Bob have listened? Or would I? Somewhat paradoxically it is one of my favourite songs.

Yes. There were people who could have told me so and chose not to. To this day, I am just not too sure who they were. I have frequently said that minding one's own business is usually the best course. I have often wondered what I would have done had I known something that could change a momentous decision another person was about to make. I have not been put to that test, so I do not know the answer. But I do wish someone had found a way to tell me that my girlfriend went offside a mere two weeks after I left the country. It might have changed a few lives for the better.

When I look again at the words of that song I know they would have been just as appropriate had there been no pregnancy. Of course we would have parted. Of course she would have cheated. Yes, she would have left me. Jimmy van Heusen also wrote *Love and Marriage* and that was not to be our song.

She died in her sleep in her twenties. She did not deserve such a short life. She left behind a daughter who bore my name and to fully appreciate how that came to pass you need to understand this adolescent, repressed, sanctimonious, hypocritical, abusive, church-dominated, small-minded, respectability-obsessed, toxic island at the West of Europe where nothing was as it seemed. Change was in the air but this was still the Ireland of the Mother and Baby homes, of being read from the altar, where the real rulers were the clerics, and the politicians, like everybody else, kissed the ring the Bishop proffered. Coming from a Protestant background, and already an Atheist, I was not directly subjected to any of these beliefs, but one could not help being surrounded by their pervasive and pernicious influence.

Regrets. I have a few ...

SURVIVAL

For reasons I do not recall, the notion of hiding the pregnancy and giving up the child for adoption was never even thought about. Now married, we made a pact to tell nobody, not even our parents or anyone in our families, about the truth we both now knew. I was not the father and we agreed to go our separate ways after the baby was born. It all came under the heading of having caused enough upset already. We lived in a rented house in Dublin and more or less played house. I have no recollection of us sharing a bed but we must have. I can remember the bedroom with a double bed. I have no memory of having sex but I suspect we did. I escaped to Trinity during the day and then worked in a petrol station each night until ten o'clock. I think we both felt we were living out a sentence. I don't remember any fights or unpleasantness. I do remember taking her to a very expensive restaurant in town one Saturday night. We got the bus to Dawson Street and spent about a month's petrol station money on one meal. We must have looked a very out of place young couple among the Dublin business community. I wore a green suede jacket, and she always looked good, so we hoped they might think we were visiting pop stars. After the meal we waited at the bus stop again to be returned to Churchtown, while I assume everyone else got into a Merc or Jag.

I recall being at college the day she went into labour and carrying on as normal and feigning disinterest while she gave birth alone in Holles Street. Perhaps her sister was with her. I am not a cruel person but I must have been mentally withdrawing and preparing to separate. I have a memory of an infant lying on that double bed and looking at her as she smiled up at me, but no recollection of ever holding her. We named her Áine Patricia after my mother and another woman I greatly admired. I find this hard to understand today but perhaps we were still maintaining a facade. Those names were definitely my choices. Maybe for some fleeting days or weeks it was difficult to face up to parting. We may have wondered if we could make it work. If so, that did not last long. One person has told me it was at the christening, which I cannot remember, that the full story broke. They were astonished to learn I had known for more than six months. We parted as we had planned. She went back to Kilkenny. I was looking forward to the summer and had already booked my flight to America.

After the baby was born we did make some enquiries about adoption but that was a non-runner. I suspect both families would have welcomed this as a solution as it was clear neither of us was ready to be a parent. I was interviewed in an office in Merrion Square. The sympathetic woman who conducted the interview, a highly regarded lawyer whom I recognised and remember well, must have thought I cut a pathetic lost figure. There was nothing they could do. In the Ireland of that time a legitimate child could not be adopted. Since we had married the child bore my name, was my child, and I was recorded as father on her birth certificate. She was not illegitimate, a concept thankfully since abolished, and so ineligible for adoption.

By early summer I was back with my college friends on another J1 visa, continuing my love affair with the USA. That year it was in Cambridge Massachusetts and, with a dreadful lack of originality, working in another ice factory with a few of the same people as the previous year and doing the night shift from midnight to 8 am once again. Jobs for Irish students were handed on from year to year. Our focus once again was money. A high point of the day was buying a dozen Dunkin' Donuts between us when we got off the subway and getting an extra one free. We lived a bit, but not a lot, better than year one. Despite Cambridge being a student town, with Harvard and MIT down the road, there seemed to have been more to do free in Washington DC. Nothing even remotely romantic, or lustful, happened that summer. I was closed down. I can remember quite a bit about the previous summer in Washington DC but virtually nothing of that summer in Boston. My wife and baby Áine remained in Kilkenny, probably trying to figure out how best to deal with the circumstances. I had exited both lives and had little interest in the opposite sex for the remainder of my undergraduate years at TCD.

There is one thought that has haunted me over the years. Could it all have been any different? Most likely not. The determinist in me says these were the hands we were dealt. As young philosophy and psychology students we spent many college hours arguing about free will, and to this day I have not resolved that argument with myself. In many ways it is as pointless as discussing a world where the bullet missed JFK or the Omagh bomb failed to explode. Or a world where Mick Jagger got fat and Pavarotti didn't, a planet where Tiger Woods only drove golf balls and not cars. Thinking about what could have been for other people is an intellectual game. When you are thinking about yourself it feels a lot different. It doesn't matter what my views on free will are. We know the sun will collapse in about six billion years and nothing will matter much then in any case. It is a thought I find a touch chilling but in the meantime I feel free, the sun is in the sky, and I do feel that things could have been different.

Some of the regrets I have are very general and difficult to pin down. There is one that is very real and I can easily see was a direct result of the teenage mess. When I was doing my PhD I was fortunate to have a very good relationship with a talented science student who also went on to get her PhD. There was a lot about the relationship that worked, and she was not bothered by the events of the previous years. She took them for what they were. A mess and a screw up. It could have happened to anyone. She didn't dwell on it. Her mother, by contrast did, and was hell-bent on seeing the back of me. She wanted a lot better for her daughter and certainly not someone who came with my back-story. Opposition like that only drives you closer. Under normal circumstances there is a reasonable chance we would have married and it would have been a good marriage. She did go on to have a happy marriage, family and good career. But I was not normal. Something in me made me sabotage the happiness that was in front of me. In short I did not feel worthy of her. I only deserved punishment.

I did have one earlier skirmish with intimacy. After my finals, which were the only exams to happen in May, I went to upstate New York to work on a very run-down golf course. There I met a very attractive Lebanese American woman who was studying ecology, a subject that had not yet made any appearance in my part of the world, but which fitted in well with my whole earth approach to our planet. We got on well and she transferred to TCD for an academic year when I began as a postgrad. The affair didn't go the distance and she returned to the US at the end of the year. She went on to have a child and happy relationship and we have since met up occasionally in New York. Thankfully I did not spread the damage to her.

So did it mess up my life? Or to put it more precisely, to what extent and in what ways did it mess up my life? I had settled back into life in Trinity College and got my degree in Philosophy and Psychology, or Mental and Moral Science as it was quaintly called, and began work for a PhD. I did have some girlfriends but none of any seriousness. It is not that easy to mention casually that you had a quick marriage in the not too distant past. There is no right time to bring that up in conversation. If you don't mention it you could be accused of being deceptive. If you do, it implies a level of seriousness that neither of you are feeling, and that is inappropriately soon in a college relationship. Let's just say you are less likely to be brought home to meet the parents for Sunday dinner. There is too much of a whiff of unnecessary danger about you. In any case no one is interested in your explanations. Looked at in another way, would I have come home for Sunday lunch with my parents, bringing my new girlfriend with me, a classmate who had already achieved a marriage break-up and baby before twenty? I don't think they would have been thrilled. What's sauce for the goose etc. That is not any crazy prejudice. It is just common sense and would raise a few eyebrows even today. If having a good straightforward life is hard enough there is no need to make it even more difficult.

In 1973 when I got my primary degree there weren't a lot of jobs around. I did apply for one Health Board job in an institution for severely intellectually disabled people in need of full-time care. I was asked in the interview how I felt about taking them to Mass every day and I replied something along the lines that I thought there were more important things that could be done to enhance their quality of life. That was the end of that.

I had got a good enough degree to get a liveable grant so I stayed on in Trinity, did some part time teaching, which was the norm, and got a PhD in the fullness of time. I remember those years with fondness. I was part of a group of good friends with inquisitive minds and a fairly counterculture but scientific approach to life. Behaviour was a subject for scientific study and we recorded all sorts of data. I have a photo of a sign on the wall reminding us of the importance of honest positive reinforcement which, even today, I would not hugely disagree with. We abolished birthdays and appointed one of us to draw up a table of random interval present days so we never knew when our substitute birthday was. Thankfully Hallmark never took this idea up. I loved those four years.

The Column I Never Wrote

In 1977, with PhD more or less completed, I applied for a lectureship in what was then University College Galway and, to my surprise, got the job. That says something about where my confidence was. When the professor later told me in an indiscreet moment that I was first choice by a mile, I found it impossible to believe. Imposter syndrome and insecurity had well and truly taken hold and are occasional companions to this day. That year of teaching enthusiastic students a few years younger than me was fantastic. A well-established lecturer in Sociology, Michael D Higgins, was very kind to me. I have never lost respect for the importance of teaching. It is a skill and an attitude you can use in myriad ways through life. I admire good teachers and have never had any time for the bad ones who damage kids each year and cannot be fired. They would be happier elsewhere and so would the pupils. It is a societal scandal that has never ceased to annoy me.

After a year in Galway, and on the verge of buying a rural cottage, for no better reason than it was what people did then, once you were a paid-up member of the permanent and pensionable trap, I moved back to Dublin. Once again I was completely surprised to be selected for a similar job on the permanent and pensionable lecturing staff in TCD. I had only been away for a year and a half. If golf was my first obsession in life then psychology was the next, with a good helping of music thrown in. To be paid to teach psychology to intelligent students, and have plenty of time to read and discuss, was almost too good to be true. In that short time most of my contemporaries had already moved abroad. Trinity was, and I am sure still is, crammed full of interesting bright people with inquisitive minds. I stayed in that job for five years, all of which I loved. I did normal things like buy a heavily-mortgaged house and get a car loan, now I had a salary.

I began writing for newspapers and magazines and, without realising it, that was to be the foundation for the next stage in my life. A prominent *Irish Times* journalist called Mary Maher got in touch. She had a Friday page which in those days was the women's page. She wanted to increase the coverage of psychology but not in a psychobabble way. Paul Tansey, also of the *Irish Times*, who I knew very slightly, had suggested my name. Mary and I sat down for an Indian lunch and by the end of it had sketched out eight articles. We did a lot more than that original eight over the next two years and I began to value the thirty quid for the *Irish Times* piece more than my Trinity salary. I liked the clear relationship between words and money. Then Anne Harris became editor of *Image* and asked me to write some provocative, humorous sort of psychological pieces, something I loved doing. Soon after, her sister, Mary O Sullivan asked me to go on *The Late Late Show* representing Divorce Action Group. I spoke once for about a minute and was pretty awful. But I had got the media bug. I loved the immediacy of it. And it was usually an opportunity to popularise psychology which I very much wanted to do. Would any of this have happened had I not had my life derailed some years earlier? Probably not. Would I have developed it with more confidence and purpose? Probably.

After five years working in TCD I heard a radio ad once, and once only, that aroused my curiosity. I applied for the job and some months later I was offered a six month contract as a trainee television Producer/Director at RTE. This time I didn't feel a fraud because I had no idea what it entailed. It was an opportunity, an experiment. Prof Barbara Wright, Dean of Arts, could not have been more supportive. She told me Trinity was always pleased to see graduates working in important places and RTE fitted the bill. She agreed to hold my job open for a year in case things didn't work out. I hugely appreciated that freedom.

My mother thought I was mad to give up a permanent and pensionable job at Trinity, which was ever so respectable and where I was wearing a tweed jacket, for the insecurity of a six month contract with the national broadcaster. I spent fifteen very happy years in RTE, travelled a lot of the world working, got to know an Ireland I had not known existed, replaced my obsession with psychology with obsession about television, and after a very fulfilling stint in Current Affairs ended up producing *The Late Late Show* with Gay Byrne. The word genius is used casually, but he met all of the criteria. And as a plus was a wonderful human being. One is very lucky in life if your path crosses with even one remarkable person.

RTE gets a slagging today, just as it always has done. People who have left, myself included, go on about how much better it was in their day. RTE and the broadcasting landscape have changed enormously in the last twenty years. For me to go back there today would probably feel as foreign as going back to TCD, or even school. There is just so much more media that the dominance of any one sector reduces. RTE does however retain a unique place in our society. There are not many places where you will walk into the canteen and meet more creative intelligent people who are either working there or visiting to contribute to a programme. RTE has an Access All Areas pass to the country. Camera crews, researchers, reporters are invited into every aspect of the country and that builds up a huge store of cultural knowledge. People will say you don't see that on air, but I always find myself defending the institution when I hear that. When I joined RTE I had probably been in less than half of our counties and often just passing through. It wasn't long before I had slept in every county and that is an enriching privilege. After a typical few weeks of meeting millionaires and paupers, achievers and wannabees, unions and workers, crooks and saints, glue sniffers and rock stars, AIDS sufferers to religious freaks and do gooders, one cannot but develop a deeper understanding of the country and a tolerance for the rich tapestry of life. Of course lots of people meet people from all walks of life. But I am still inclined to think a big media organisation has unique tentacles.

So no. My life was not a disaster. I survived, though work is a limited measure of a human life. I am confident that if you had asked me back then if the deception, marriage, birth and subsequent parting had any effect on me I would have replied they were long forgotten. I may even have believed it. I would not have been telling the full truth because, even then, I knew I had a lot of demons who were more in charge of me than I was of them. That is not how it should have been.

In reflective moments I might have commented that after my late teen trauma I never had a child, nor ever had the slightest desire to do so. I remember the Late Late programme secretary telling me one day that she thought I would make a great father. Little did she know what memories I was harbouring. But then some of my close friends never had children either. It is a decision some perfectly happy and fulfilled couples make. I remember one friend telling me that he and his wife knew there would probably be times in their lives when they would regret not having children, but they felt they were making the right decision for them. They are still together and very happy with their lot.

I have occasionally admitted to myself that I always had difficulties with intimacy. I would place a woman on a pedestal, enjoy the chase, but once the feeling was reciprocated I began the slow process of closing down my emotions until the other person had the common sense to end it. Yes, I was hurt now and again, but never with anything like the fundamental ferocity of that teenage deception. Not within a mile of it. I was always ready to dust myself off and start all over again. I never allowed myself become that vulnerable again. My pattern became to withdraw, become, or behave, depressed, and act with so little interest that I was eventually dumped, or things fizzled out. That suited me fine. There were those who commented that I always protected myself by having someone waiting in the wings to fill the spot and there is probably more truth in that than I care to admit. There were a few chances of a good relationship, a relationship that, had I a different back story, might have become a successful marriage, but I balked at each. Perhaps it is not quite that black and white as there are always two people involved, but there is way more than a grain of truth. When you have something big in your past a relationship cannot develop at a normal, or appropriate, pace. In retrospect I should have left Ireland and begun afresh elsewhere, probably in America.

I never ever had a vision of a happy family, such as the one I grew up in, as being an aspiration or at all possible. I sometimes think of it as the curse of growing up with very happy parents. It sets an impossibly high standard, particularly so as the certainties of life diminish with each generation, and the opportunities of life become even more complex. I marvel at any marriage that lasts more than a decade now. When you have parents who chat to each other into the small hours of the morning, and whose faces light up when the other appears, most other relationships look second best. I recall watching Fr Feargal O'Connor on *The Late Late Show* during one of our divorce referenda. He said that, in his experience, in only about ten per cent of marriages were the two partners the absolute centre of each other's lives. My parents were in that small group. Ten per cent, he said, couldn't stand each other, and the remaining eighty per cent got on fine but could probably replace the partner without too much difficultly if the need arose. He was also asked a question about how long he thought it took for people to get over the experience of a marriage ending. He answered with a simple question. How long were they married? he asked. That is how long it will take. Someone in the audience had asked what would a celibate priest know about marriage. He knew more than most of them put together. In the case of the short traumatic marriage I had gone through I suspect he would have multiplied the recovery time by ten. Or twenty.

Relationships are of many types and don't all have to go the distance. I have a picture by an artist friend, with whom I was once close, that reminds me there are a lot of great people out there and the trick in life is to appreciate them when you have the opportunity. I have several of her paintings and my favourite one is of U2 leaving the stage at a London concert we had gone to together. It takes a lot of explanation for the viewer but it is worth it when they figure it out. She always saw things in her unique way.

I never drive the dual carriageway past RTE without thinking of this magical woman.

I had collected her in town and was driving her to Dún Laoghaire. At the red lights in Donnybrook she began to tell me her day's work had been to get started on a portrait of me. I was part amazed and fully flattered and immediately began to ask a host of questions. Had she a photo? Did I need to sit? How could she manage from memory? The lights had changed and we had gone about a quarter of a mile when she explained that: Oh, it isn't your face. It's your penis.

She gave it to me for my birthday. It still hangs, and hanging is very much the wrong word, outside my bedroom and gives me a regular laugh. It is not a great testament to her memory but it is a great tribute to her imagination. She told me she had done six versions. I trust the others found their way into dustbins.

DNA

Despite the absence of divorce in Ireland in the 1970s, I was able to achieve the feat of having an ex-wife. She had moved to London, leaving her pre-school daughter in Ireland to be cared for by her family. I was not consulted, nor should I have been. It was further and public acceptance that I was not the father.

Time had moved on and she needed a fresh start and that would not have been realistic with a very young child in tow. I am sure she was heartily sick of the sidelong glances and the well-meaning gossips that poison every provincial town. Every community has plenty of Johnnypatteenmikes that were portrayed so wonderfully by Martin McDonagh in *The Cripple of Inishmaan*. The town was the right size for the gossip and their audience to meet and swap the scandal. When I was working in University College Galway an academic once told me with a wry smile that the university politics were much more vicious in that institution because there weren't enough issues and jobs to go around. When I walk through NUIG now, and see the massive changes and huge development, I often think of that man!

We were not able to have the marriage annulled despite my wife investigating that route. It was not a concept I had any time for anyway. This is a church concept and to say a marriage had not taken place seemed absurd. No one forced anyone, thought it could be argued I did not have the full facts. It would have made no difference as the state law took precedence over church law. With the help of a talented Kilkenny solicitor that my father spoke to we got divorced after she moved to England and we had lived apart, she in England and me in Dublin, for two years. I still have the correspondence. The solicitor knew I was paying, and was still a student. He charged me the princely sum of twelve pounds. There are kindnesses that happen throughout life and they need to be remembered and appreciated. If I learned one thing from this awful mess it is that when someone is in difficulty a small act of kindness is enormous. It must have been one of the earliest divorces that applied in this jurisdiction as Ireland recognised UK divorces. I have a recollection that I went out with a few friends to celebrate, which was probably just a bit of exhibitionism on my part. Some part of me thought a divorce party was a bit hippyish, and it was a first for me. Not an achievement anyone else wanted but that didn't matter.

We had now parted formally and were in different countries. In time my ex-wife began another relationship and we had no further contact, now the divorce had been worked out. I did meet her once, several years later, while shopping in Capel Street on a Saturday afternoon. We spotted each other from about twenty yards. She was carrying a child in a sling. Both our faces lit up and we walked straight to each other and into a massive bear hug until we realised we were in danger of squashing the poor infant. We held each other and looked at each other and I can't remember what we said but it was warm and friendly. It was all over in a few minutes. It was the last time I saw her and I am glad it happened. She was not a bad person and the light was still on in her eyes. Sadly her short life was nearing its end.

The girlfriend I was with at the time went into a sulk that lasted a lot longer than the hug. How could you even look at her? she demanded. Repeatedly. That put a fairly solid nail in that coffin. Life is never simple. Maybe she was right to be angry, or jealous. Looking back, were it not for the child in her sling, and possibly the father beside her, though I don't recall him, we would probably have run off for the weekend together without giving it a second thought. There is a song Cat Stevens wrote and PP Arnold made immortal – *The First Cut is the Deepest* – and there is a lot of truth in it. It can be very difficult to ever love like that again. Today how many people have googled old lovers and wondered about getting back in touch despite being quite happy where they are? Very dangerous. I suggest you give it a miss. Fantasy can be so much more attractive than reality. And it is just that. Fantasy.

It was while working in RTE that I first met Áine again. I was filming in the North West and, as happens, word goes round when RTE are in town. I got a phone call to the hotel from my ex-wife's older brother. Could we meet? I was delighted to. It turned out that Áine, now a teenager, was being raised by her uncle and his wife. They had welcomed her to be part of their family, a gesture of kindness which she always appreciated. He and I met and he was keen to compare our recollections of the events of some fifteen years earlier. By and large our memories concurred. Like me he recalled that the chances of me being her father were pretty much zero. That was also what Áine had been told. He thought she was keen to meet me in any case and he was comfortable for me to meet with her. We met the next day.

She asked me a lot of questions, mostly about her mother who had died several years earlier. She was a bubbly amiable teenager. We liked each other from the off. She was full of personality and had a strong look of her mother. I had to resist almost staring at her to see if anything of me looked back. It didn't. A few years after that meeting she left school and she moved to London. She would get in touch with me whenever she was in Ireland, maybe once or twice a year. I would meet her for coffee if I was in London. She got in touch with me before she married as she wanted me to meet the man in question. That marriage did not work out. She got in touch again, in her thirties, to tell me she was marrying again. Thankfully that marriage was very successful and she got the happiness due to her. There was a link of sorts between us and I would update her on what I was up to and vice versa. I was an avuncular person, semi-detached from her. She laughed easily and was always fun. She came for a meal at my house in Dublin once. After she had left a woman friend, who had joined us and knew the history, said well, you can be certain she is not your daughter. Take my word for it. She was confident in what she was saying, and in any case it concurred with what I believed.

I was past one of my many mid-life buy-another-motorbike crises when Áine phoned to ask if I would take a DNA test. I had no difficulty whatsoever doing so, but the reason she asked was a very unpleasant one. She had been diagnosed with cancer and investigations showed she was a carrier of the BRCA gene, the gene Angelina Jolie made famous, which increases susceptibility to breast cancer. She had never had children, but she wanted to pass this important health information to her biological father as it might have health implications for any female children he might have had. She wanted the piece of paper in case she was met with an answer that pointed in my direction. She wanted to be able to rule me out. She did not want to trouble the wrong person with a skeleton from long ago. It seemed to me she was far more concerned with protecting other women than finding her biological father. We talked about who her father might be, as we had a few times over the years (she was now forty), and, as usual, neither of us knew. I had heard two names occasionally over the years but could never be sure what was just rumour. The memories of people I knew who were around that summer had faded and become intermixed with gossip. At one stage I thought it was one person until some months later someone told me it was another. There was confusion between two brothers. It could well have been neither of them. It was all a bit lost in the mists of time and she had never made contact with either of the probables.

A short time later she sent me the results of the DNA test which, in black and white, stated the chances of me being her father were zero per cent. For some reason I keep that document on my phone. I suspect she may have held out some little hope in some part of her mind that it might be different as, despite not having a lot of contact, we had always got on well and there was a trust between us. The result of the DNA test was not a surprise to me. Any different result would have been devastating as I would have been living a huge lie to myself and everybody else. That said, my clear recollection is my wife of five days had not said I might not be the father. She told me I wasn't the father. She didn't introduce any doubt into the situation. I don't believe she had any doubt at any time.

I was walking along the river when Áine phoned to tell me the result before forwarding the details by email. My first thought was I wished my parents were alive to have seen this definitive answer. I get fed up hearing the word closure, but I do think it would have drawn a line under the events for them. They were badly hurt. The experience had never gone away. Around the same time a friend, who knew nothing of my distant past, told me she had been told I had a child by someone who appeared to know the events of years earlier, chapter and verse. The purveyor of the information had a lot of it wrong. I did not come well out of the story. I was the Trinity student who got a nice young girl pregnant and had done a runner. I expect my parents, or more particularly my mother, suffered similar well-meaning conversations. Gossips have long memories and flimsy connections with the truth. We are all familiar with the delight such people get from bearing bad news. In the defence of such carriers of news it seems likely the history was rewritten a number of times, not least because the young woman I married had died so young. What happened next demolished any notion that I had dealt with the events of those distant years.

My daughter, for in law and on her birth certificate she always was my daughter and used my name, phoned me again, maybe a week or two later.

She had continued in her quest to accurately identify the father. I think she had some genetic counselling as she seemed very well versed in the risks to the females who would be her blood relations. What was troubling her that day, and she was very angry, was the number of people who were able to give her information about the events of some forty years ago, information that was helpful to her. If they had ever harboured any doubts, then the results of that test removed them and people talked freely to her. Her conversation and texts to me were a variety of forms of why did no one tell me, mixed with why did no one tell you? For the duration of the calls I was the calming influence. She was furious. It was one of the last conversations we were ever to have.

That evening I began about six months of angst, ruminating about what my life could have been, raging at miscellaneous people who let me go through with the sham marriage, embarrassment at what a fool people must have thought I was, and, surprisingly, affection for the woman who had put me through it. She was caught in a trap. She was not a bad person. We never had the opportunity to ever discuss it maturely. She was probably the only person who could have brought clarity, and even comfort. Talking to her was out of the question as she had been dead some thirty years.

Somewhere out there, should he still be alive, is the person who actually is Áine's father. Where was that person the day I walked up the aisle? Had they been contacted by her when she realised she was pregnant? If so how had they reacted? Maybe they had told her to go to hell. Maybe not. It seems unlikely that, in this small gossipy country, word did not reach them that she was pregnant. And getting married. Could he have not heard that piece of news? The most appropriate feeling I should have towards that person would be strong anger. It would be a good indication that I was psychologically healthy. But I have never felt that. I don't know if it was a big romance or a one-night stand. I don't know if it was drunk or sober. And I don't care. And never will.

It was as if my mainspring had broken. Nothing made much sense. Nothing mattered. There were nights I stared at the television. There were nights I drank myself into oblivion, though thankfully I have a stop button that kicks in after one or two of those. I don't think I ever drank to dull pain. I drank to stop thinking, to turn off my brain, to stop the woodpecker in my head. I felt a failure. I felt a fraud. At times when I had the company of someone I could trust I droned on endlessly. I felt I had wasted my life and completely underachieved because of what had happened years earlier. My ability to concentrate disappeared. I could do what was on my list. I could meet a deadline. But as regards making things happen I wasn't at the races. That hurt. One of the nicest compliments I was ever paid was by a Production Assistant in RTE who told me she loved being part of my team because I made things happen. She had no idea how much those few words meant to me. If she could have seen the state I was in, in those months, she would have been disappointed.

More than anything I wanted to sit down and talk to my mother about it but that was not possible. I wanted to talk to my one-time wife but that was also impossible. I would have liked to talk so much more to Áine about it but by then her cancer was progressing. I think she made some efforts to make contact with her father. I don't know if she was successful or not, but I think not. She soon became very ill and her husband, whom she adored, looked after her wonderfully. One day a short while later I got a phone call from a relation of hers. She had passed away, in her early forties. I felt as if another anchor that had been holding me back, or holding me in a place of some security, had been removed. I was adrift. I was so sad about the hand she had been dealt. When I should have been feeling sorry for her I was feeling sorry for myself. I was angry, confused, and without any feeling of a centre to my life that made sense.

Nothing really mattered much to me. Nothing really mattered at all.

DREAMS

Self-praise is no praise. Is self-therapy any good or is it an equally poor substitute for the real thing? Clearly, in the wake of the unambiguous DNA test, I was a psychological mess. Even I could see that, and I would be very good at denial. Would it be better to swallow my pride and bare my psychological wounds to a qualified person who is more objective than I am? I did give it some thought. Instead, I chose to write this down and take my mind back to events both recent and long gone and try and deal with them truthfully.

One or two people had been encouraging, even badgering, me to put pen to paper and deal with the demons those who know me well said still loomed too large. They thought it might be my way of dealing with it. I had a long-standing invitation to write about the events and my subsequent reaction for the *Sunday Independent* but it never felt like the right format or time. I always thought a few thousand words would raise as many questions as it would answers. And until relatively recently Áine was alive and, although she was living in London, I didn't want to drag her into it. She had had enough to deal with for one person and finally seemed to have found some happiness. It is not something I ever discussed with her. She would probably have said to go ahead.

Some people have long been telling me I needed to get therapy. If I had a euro for every time I was told that if I had a broken leg I would go to the doctor etc, etc. Most of us are not good at seeing our own demons.

Others may see them a lot more clearly. We have incorporated them in our thinking, our way of approaching life. It is like learning to live with a limp. Everyone else is aware of it.

This isn't quite the first time I have put pen to paper on this topic, but it is the first time I have done so with the knowledge that it will be read by other people and that I need to be honest with myself. Anyone who writes will tell you this is a very different task to journaling or keeping a diary. Putting it all out there is much closer to sitting down in the book-lined room and telling it to another human being.

Loneliness, or perhaps sadness, and regular nightmares were the first outcomes as I began the task. These were feelings it was easier to feel alone than to talk through with a therapist. I began to have some trust in what I was doing. I hadn't felt so alone since I was an eleven-year-old in boarding school, trying to cope with being away from home for the first time. Back then I cried my eyes out. And ran away twice. The first time I was barely five weeks in the place and living in the boarding house in Burlington Road. It was home for 24 eleven- and twelve-year-old boys. Each afternoon after school we returned there and changed out of uniform. Once I had my blazer off and brown tweed jacket on, I went outside and climbed over the wall to freedom. I made my way, crying my eyes out, to the 48A bus stop and went to a house opposite Milltown Golf Club and arrived, hysterical, at my aunt's door. She can't have been best pleased to see me but was the very essence of kindness. She calmed me down and made some phone calls. The one to my parents was long-distance, and in the daytime. These were the days when you did not make long-distance phone calls and never before 6pm unless there was something close to nuclear war. The phone bill inspired a terror far worse than leaving the immersion on. I was returned to the school and my parents advised to stick it out and that I would settle down.

As a very homesick eleven-year-old in class, I believe the next day I recall a pious matronly English teacher referring to me in front of the class as a streak of misery. I assume my adventure was the talk of the staff room. No teacher should be so thoughtlessly cruel. She also taught me to hate poetry and I regret how much pleasure I missed before I managed to get over that. She tried to turn us on to art but her taste was a bit chocolate box for me. John Constable was her hero. Even if you gave me *The Hay Wain* I wouldn't hang it on my wall. Maybe I am being hard on him but not on her. Incidentally, the last of Constable's paintings in private hands, *The Lock*, sold for 22.4 million sterling at Christie's in London in 2012, so maybe that teacher knew more than I thought.

I did settle down to an extent. My parents must have been driven demented. In reality from a Protestant perspective there was no alternative to Dublin schooling. Back then Kilkenny College only taught to Intermediate Certificate. Perhaps Newtown in Waterford was an option, and the Quaker ethos might have suited me, but it wasn't considered. To have sent me to a Kilkenny Catholic school in those days would not have been an option.

I ran away a second time some months later. With a startling lack of originality I jumped over the same wall, took the same bus and arrived at the same unfortunate aunt's door. The only difference was this time I had to take five minutes at the end of the road to work myself into a state as I was actually enjoying the escapade. I was probably just attention-seeking this time. Even back then I liked to get my way. Once again I was dispatched back to prison in a few hours. I always think of that day when anyone says the definition of stupidity is doing the same thing over and over and expecting a different result. My parents drove to Dublin that night fully prepared to bring me home and work something out. Apparently they came into our six person dorm. All of us were sleeping peacefully and they decided to leave well enough alone. By this stage I was broken. I never escaped, or even thought about it, again. I had been told I would be expelled and that was a very heavy threat.

As it happened I did get expelled in the long run and have kept the letter. That was nearly six years later and I had already passed the TCD matriculation exams and been accepted. I didn't need to sit the Leaving Cert and that spelled trouble. The devil makes work for idle hands. I was bound to cause trouble. My mother often said the main difference between me and some others was I always got caught. This time it was for riding a motorbike without tax, insurance, a licence or much ability. That was enough. They got rid of me. I wasn't too bothered. While others prepared for the Leaving Cert I played golf. It would be only two years later that I would give those self-righteous teachers all the proof they needed that they were right all along. I was a no good.

Half a century later, bringing these events to mind brought no tears. Just a feeling of aloneness that made me think of George Clooney in his space suit in Gravity, drifting off alone into infinity and eternity, and without Sandra Bullock. This time there was no sanctimonious teacher to categorise or add to my distress. I just sat there looking at the muted television, observing myself in my aloneness. I was how I imagined a ghost to be if it chose to return to its home from a later life. If someone had walked in the door, and there was no possibility of that for I was at home alone, I may as well have been invisible. I certainly felt very insignificant in this vast universe. Thinking of infinity is not good for one's mental health. German mathematician Georg Cantor, who dreamed up set theory, spent his waking hours thinking of infinite numbers and apparently resided much of his adult life in mental hospitals as a result. If you are going through an existential crisis it is probably best to leave infinity alone. Just look at the sky in wonder and have a cup of tea. You are already feeling insignificant enough. I often wonder how Brian Cox keeps so happy because he, better than most of us, knows how truly insignificant we are.

In 1977 Voyager 1 embarked from NASA on a long trip into space to study our solar system. In 1990, from six billion miles away, a photo was taken where earth can be seen as a tiny pale blue dot. This is how we might appear to others, were there others out there. Scientist Carl Sagan saw this picture as a wonderful demonstration of the folly of any human conceit. He pointed out that we humans are inhabiting one rock together and it is up to us to realise none of us is special and we should deal more kindly with each other and do our best to preserve this home we have. I have that photo and Sagan's quote on my fridge. It is a good thought to have at some time every day. Today Voyager 1 is the most distant man-made object from earth at 14.1 billion miles. If it could be lonely, it should be.

Loneliness is a distinct feeling and I mean it when I say I had not experienced it since childhood. I spent a lot more time than normal alone during the 20/21 lockdowns, but I never experienced any loneliness because of that. I was quite content, if at times a bit bored. Loneliness does not normally seem to play much part in my make-up. It wasn't what I felt when my parents died and I was with each of them as they drew their last breath. My mother died very reluctantly. It was a mere nine weeks after her cancer diagnosis. She was not ready and was angry. One moment of levity came about a month after the diagnosis when she won a car on Mike Murphy's Winning Streak with a ticket my sister had bought. Mike was very kind to her. He knew she was ill. She talked about fighting it. We knew she would not win. So did she. She was a nurse. For months, after she died, the only two pieces of music I could listen to were Mozart's *Requiem* and *Achtung Baby*. Everything else sounded trite and irritating.

My father was more prepared for death. He was eighty-five and his health was declining. Some years earlier he had a pacemaker fitted. As he lay dying, there were several times when we thought he was gone and the pacemaker would kick in. Eventually we all ended up laughing hysterically and told him to get on with it. He did.

Compared to loneliness, grief is a much more complicated mix of emotions, from relief to sadness and anger, to physical pain and uncontrollable tears. We learn the bones of it as children when a pet dies. Loneliness, that feeling of being lost and yearning for an undefined something, is what I felt after I wrote down my memories of the teenage events as had been suggested to me. Sitting looking out to the ocean can make one feel very insignificant but in a positive way. You see yourself as a small thing connected to everything else, each of which has its part to play. When lonely, one does not feel connected to anything. I could have left the universe without causing a ripple.

Loneliness is a different feeling from that experienced after the break-up of a romance. That also is a cluster of feelings from regret to anger to relief. It contains all of the ego-driven what will people think emotions, from embarrassment to shame. How could she do this? To ME !!!! There may be lots of jealous feelings of the partner being with someone else, no matter who initiated the break-up. In some instances, if the person walked in the door with a smile, all would be reversed in seconds.

Loneliness is not like that. If the phone had rung I might not have answered. If I did I would have faked it and said I was in good form. Automatic pilot is easy. It was not a time to talk. I had spilled out all I could say for the time being. I was empty. Most nights I wouldn't have touched a glass of wine. I wanted to feel the emotion I was feeling purely, without interference. On the nights I did drink I drank too much, happy to bring on oblivion. That aloneness may well have been a feeling that had been waiting for close to fifty years to be noticed. It needed to take its time.

I was not looking for company. Not only will loneliness not disappear with the presence of another person or with a kind touch, but I suspect such supposed comforts would have made things worse. They would have felt like an intrusion, and I would have been certain no one could have understood. If someone had tried to offer consolation I would have become irritable. What had happened hadn't happened to them. I know now how people can become very isolated and those around them may not be aware of it. I was lonely and I wanted to keep it that way. I wanted to be as alone as it was possible to be, and that doesn't mean to wallow in it. Rather just to be in it for as long as it required me to be. It was almost reassuring, like being visited by an old long forgotten friend. I felt safe. I felt calm.

The Irish author, John Boyne, wrote movingly in the *Irish Times* around the time a teacher from his former secondary school had been jailed for abusing pupils. John had not been a victim of that man. Paradoxically he had received some encouragement in his writing from him. But he had been badly beaten by a priest and molested by a different lay teacher. It was the sexual intrusion that stayed with him to this day. He still finds himself wondering *if the first person to touch me had not been a middle-aged man in a position of authority ... would I have evolved differently, my mind less discomfited by intimacy...?* Sometimes you read words and it is as if you hear yourself talking. My experience was nothing like his in terms of abuse. I was never abused, sexually or physically, at any stage of my life. But sex was at the centre of the deception I suffered and I am inclined to think sex brings with it the energy to fuel a lifetime of confused thoughts. For a species to survive, sexual behaviour needs to be driven by a strong instinct. If it wasn't deep in our hard wiring, we as a species would not be here. John Boyne summed up, saying that abusers leave us with a history of self-loathing, failed relationships, and the last bit is contained in the title of his book *A History of Loneliness*. He was telling it as it is, without a hint of exaggeration. I felt for him. And I felt less alone. I have never met him but I felt I would like him.

Loneliness becomes normal. The separateness from other people is the only connection you understand. It made sense that loneliness was the strongest thing I felt, having put pen to paper, because that was what had been ahead of me all those years earlier – a lifetime of hidden or covered up loneliness that I would not understand. It never pained me or troubled me. It was normal. It was how I lived, with emotions punctuated by a laugh, some conversation, or work, but always followed by a return to the same emptiness, and never more so than after yet another attempt at intimacy, finally hoping the vulnerability that comes with intimacy could happen. If it ever did it was short-lived. There were times when it fooled me, but mostly it restricted me to arms-length closeness.

For me it was a totally unexpected outcome of reliving the events in some detail and taking my time about it. I was writing for an hour or two most days. There was no part of a lifetime, with the habit of introspection and self-analysis, that made me in any way prepared for this to happen. I don't know if I was longing for anything, or if that even makes sense. Each night I enjoyed watching the flickering of the fire and the warmth. If I could have tolerated the company of anybody it would have been my mother and she has been dead twenty-five years. That said, I probably wouldn't even have admitted to her what I was feeling. When you have a lifetime of putting a brave face on things, and passed the gold standard in suppressing feelings as a trapped nineteen-year-old, it is not easy to change. I never listened to music. Not even Mozart or U2 would have reached me. In the small hours of the morning I went to bed, stone cold sober most nights, sozzled occasionally.

At times in my life I have had vivid nightmares. They began soon after I broke up with Áine's mother. Back then they only ever happened when I felt completely safe, and never when I was alone in a house. That meant, for many years, they only occurred at weekends when I was sleeping in my old bed in my parents' house, the very same bed in the very same room where I had looked down from my out-of-body self. My mother often told me she heard me screaming during the night. I remember waking up in terror but I do not remember anything of the dreams and did not write them down which, since I was a psychology student, I find slightly surprising.

As the years passed the intensity and frequency of the night terrors declined, while the number of places where I felt secure enough to endure a bad dream increased. When I was working it happened in hotels. For years I had a recurring dream of desperately trying to find an old car I had bought, an antique Rolls Royce or Model T Ford, but never being able to locate it. It doesn't sound frightening, but it was very unsettling. For the last twenty years I have a recurring dream of coming back to the house I live in and it has been taken over by about a hundred chaotic people who do not see me and I cannot make myself seen. Again it is unsettling, but not terribly frightening. Since writing this down a different and much more intense one has taken its place.

The phone number of the house where my parents lived in Kilkenny from when I was seven years old was 056 - 7721472. This was the house where I was told the truth that night. The phone number is like a social history of the town. When my father moved there, to open a branch of what was then the Sun Insurance, the number was Kilkenny 7. We were then living at the other side of town and I learned to count by looking at the funerals at the mortuary of St Luke's Hospital across the road. As more people got phones the number became 472 and that is the number we took with us when we moved house. Many years later the 056 and 21 were added for Kilkenny and then finally the 77 prefix was added as having a house phone had become normal. People finally had landlines, and extensions, even answering machines, all of which would be gradually replaced by wireless technology. As a child I can remember a stream of people, who had not yet got a phone, waiting in our house around Christmas and receiving calls from relatives overseas and the great excitement of it all.

Now that number is often with me at night as I desperately try to ring it in my sleep. But the buttons on my mobile will not work. It is as if they are glued together. I am all fingers and thumbs and no matter how I try I cannot complete the number before I wake up. I never get to speak to my mother. She never appears in the dream. She never knew about the DNA test. The certainty provided by the science would have mattered. That is the first recurrent dream which came to me again, having written the above. I wake up screaming, never sure if I actually am screaming or if the scream is part of the dream.

Then one night the phone is answered and I hear a male voice I don't recognise. I ask to speak to my parents. They don't live here, he tells me. I realise they are dead and wake up.

I take a fairly jaundiced view of dreams containing symbols and coded messages. I suspect dreams are either a great deal more random, or more straightforward, than that. Perhaps what a dream is saying may be staring you in the face. A conversation with a psychologist friend brought this home to me with startling simplicity. I had talked about the recurrent dream of trying to dial my mother and failing all of the time. I hadn't really focussed on the content of the dream. I was more influenced by the feeling of being trapped and of not be able to get anywhere, of huge effort with no result, and the distress of waking up. More often than not I wasn't feeling great fear. Just exhaustion and failure. But there were nights of terror and as a result I frequently lay awake, afraid sleep would bring some fresh hell. My friend listened and then asked the simplest of questions. Well, if you did get through to her, what would you say? What are you so desperate to tell her?

It was a blindingly obvious question I had never really considered properly. I could try telling her I had finally figured it all out. That it wasn't my fault at all, I was an innocent victim, that I had a horrific shock, that the result was PTSD. It stands to reason. I am not convinced what I said would have withstood her scrutiny. She had seen real victims. I would have had to convince her I wasn't a bandwagon victim.

PTSD

When I studied, taught, and for a time practiced, psychology one of the most annoying phrases I heard was, I'm a bit of a psychologist myself. The statement was usually followed by some half-baked theory based on a magazine article the speaker was attracted to because it fitted their particular interest. I am a great fan of Susie Dent who is a fixture on the TV programme *Countdown* and posts very unusual words on Twitter. I particularly liked ultracrepedarian, which even spellcheck doesn't know. It means someone who holds forth on things they know absolutely nothing about. I am not immune to this foible myself and I did find myself listening to mentions of PTSD, and even reading some books about it, preferably ones with big print that I could skim quickly. I was ready to pontificate on the subject. There was also no shortage of well-meaning armchair psychologists telling me I must have PTSD...Sure you would have to after that experience. It can't have no effect on you.

During the First World War, soldiers returned home from the most appalling situations and were said to be suffering from shell shock. It is hard to imagine what they endured and yet there appeared to be an attitude of why didn't they just get on with it when they returned home safely. They did just that. Many of them never spoke of their experiences. Old newsreel footage, or even the best made movies, cannot recreate the sheer ongoing terror of what must have been their daily norm.

Likewise the Second World War. The story of Private Eddie Slovik brings all of the horror home to me. A film about his life is one of the most harrowing I have ever watched. It reminds me, as if I needed reminding, how fortunate men of my age in this part of the world are, never to have faced war. Slovik, a twenty-four-year-old American soldier, basically lost it, having been under sustained heavy fire in France. He made it clear he just couldn't take any more and technically deserted, though he told everyone what he was doing and where to find him. It was 1945 and the war was in its final stages. Slovik was court-martialled and became the only American soldier in the Second World War to be executed for a purely military offence. It cannot have been for any other reason than some vindictive people in charge wanted to make an example of the unfortunate man. To make matters worse, the firing squad made a mess of the execution and he took fifteen minutes to die. The army wasn't very impressed by shell shock and, we can infer, would not have had a lot of time for PTSD.

I have walked around Auschwitz, pretty much in silence, but without any real visceral comprehension of what was done to people and by whom it was done. I did stand rooted in horror, looking at the actual stakes where people were tortured and hanged. I lingered in a room where unfortunates were deliberately starved to death and looked at their scrawls on the wall. It is an unusual tourist destination. The word attraction is obviously inappropriate. There is very little conversation as the crowd shuffles around the site. No laughter. I can't recall anyone being dumb enough to take a selfie, which is quite something these days. I never lost the feeling that the atrocities were done by civilised educated people to civilised educated people. In another life I could have been at a dinner table with both victim and perpetrator of these atrocities. I kept on remembering it was not that long ago, and similar horrors had since been inflicted in Rwanda, in Ethiopia, Myanmar, and nearer to home, in the Balkans. That was before my mind turned to the IRA and UVF.

I was driven back to Krakow, about an hour away, had a pleasant dinner and a good night's sleep and, to an extent, ticked another must do sometime off the list. It was the first and only time I have been in a concentration camp. During that war, and the Korean War, shell shock was replaced by the somewhat more innocuous combat fatigue. This implied that you needed a good rest and all would be well.

In Nagasaki I stood at the site of the second atomic bomb and listened to a woman who had survived it tell me about that morning on 9 August 1945 when she was a young child. Her sister, who had been standing beside her, was killed instantly. To have come that close to death probably necessitated more than a few good sleeps.

The closest I ever got to actually seeing the psychological effects of war was when I was a student and spending the summers working in America. I remember one Vietnam vet who worked in the ice factory. I don't quite know why, but we all knew it was better to keep our distance. Well in excess of 50,000 of his colleagues died and way more Vietnamese, Cambodians and Laotians died so he had seen, and possibly done, things that would leave a mark. To say he was unstable, deeply troubled, was to put it mildly. I remember him going a bit berserk one day and running up and down the yard with an imaginary gun and blasting everything in sight. He told us he was shooting gooks and in his mind he may well have been.

Then I shared a house in upstate New York with a bunch of people and one of the rooms was occupied by a very disturbed vet. He was a friend of a friend of a friend and the understanding was he had been through a tough time and needed some space to get his head back together. He spent twenty-three hours a day alone in his room. We didn't know if he read, watched TV, slept or what. No one was invited in. We were on a farm in the middle of nowhere and no one visited him so he wasn't doing drugs, though he may well have while in Asia. He emerged twice a day and cooked buckwheat pancakes and barely spoke.

It was around that time the diagnosis Post Traumatic Stress Disorder, later called Stress Syndrome, began to be used and was given its place in the psychiatric bible, the DSM, that is the *Diagnostic and Statistical Manual of Mental Disorders*. Despite the fact that I was just beginning a PhD in psychology I would just have described him as bonkers and left it at that. After I left he got into a bit of a row with one of the women. There was a fear this could turn violent and he was told to leave. No one ever heard of him again. Over the years I have often wondered what he did or saw that he was so totally unable to deal with or talk about. He was luckier than many vets in that he was given time, space and a roof over his head but that clearly was not sufficient. We hadn't come a long way from shell shock.

The origins of the term PTSD were as a result of truly horrific experiences, but if you give a psychological condition a name you can be sure people will find it and wear the badge. I don't know if you can have a bit of PTSD any more than a bit of a brain tumour, but many people who never experienced the field of battle except on a screen could soon find a bit of PTSD in their life. I don't exclude myself from this, despite the fact I have never experienced real horror except when asleep, have never been in fear for my life, and have, to this day, never experienced a shock of the magnitude of that night as a cuckolded teenager on his way to unexpected fatherhood.

Pain and shock do not, of course, have to be entirely physical, and mine was all mental. I am one of that lucky group, maybe a minority in Ireland, people who never suffered physical or sexual abuse of any sort whatsoever. In our home I remember my grandmother swiping me with a tea towel for running out on the road carelessly, but that was the extent of it. A wooden spoon was occasionally brandished but never used. In secondary school it was no different. I remember a teacher losing his temper one night and slippering a few lads quite hard but it was so rare that it stands out. They had no more than sore rear ends for ten minutes and were heroes for days. Only the headmaster was permitted to use the cane and it was so rare that, again, I can remember one instance of it being used in six years for what I thought was, then and now, unfair. A classmate was summoned and given six of the best for not trying hard enough in class. There was even a rumour that his parents had requested it. From anything I ever learned about psychology this punishment was not appropriate and, in any case, would not have the desired effect. In his defence I doubt the headmaster took any pleasure in it. He was not a cruel man, but was probably happy to have God on his side with every whack.

I am always somewhat surprised when I hear people who suffered sexual abuse talk about the pain, years later, as if it happened yesterday. It is still very much with them. I read that John Boyne article over and over. Fr Brian D'Arcy has also written about the abuse he suffered from a cleric when he was a young man. He has said that, because of it, he was never able to fully trust ever again. And then he emphasised EVER. I found that an extraordinarily strong statement and he is not a man given to exaggeration. It was just a simple honest statement of the facts of the matter.

It seems as if a dreadful experience, often repeated, has stayed with victims every day. They have not in any real sense got over it. In some cases you could quite understand if they took the opportunity to blow the perpetrator's brains out. Their lives had been ruined far more than if they had lost a leg in a battlefield explosion but lived to tell the tale.

Then there are the times when people are getting on fine and some trigger resurrects the memories of long years ago. Whenever someone talks about abuse on radio it seems to produce a new avalanche of people who were affected, but had never talked about their own abuse before. This always surprised me as it is a topic that has received an enormous amount of media exposure in recent decades. Clearly there is a lot of buried pain out there. So it is easy to see how the PTSD term is so widely used to try to understand the enduring effects of psychological and physical experiences of long ago. My trauma and stressors were in my head. Nothing was damaged apart from my self-esteem, view of the world, and perhaps ability to trust or be intimate. Wouldn't it be a bit rich to start hanging PTSD on a bit of deception and resulting decisions made before I was twenty?

Looking at the literature on PTSD is a bit like examining the Covid 19 symptoms. You'd be hard put not to find something that applied to you on an off day. But with PTSD there is no easy way to clear your mind, like taking your temperature and finding it is normal, having a cup of coffee and getting on with it. Perhaps PTSD is one of those things many of us can push to the background while we get on with living. Maybe there is something to be said for the Jeremy Clarkson approach of just picking yourself up and getting on with it … a sort of broken leg? Sure 'tis only a scratch attitude. Bottle it up, man.

It never let me miss a deadline. I rarely turned up late. And I would have an existential crisis if I did not get out of bed soon after daylight at the latest. So I was far from shell shocked. Yet when I go through the symptoms it is not that I recognise them, it is more that I wonder would life have been different were it not for that betrayal.

I feel very much at home with the symptom list. I don't need to put it on the fridge door to remember it. It begins with flashbacks which do not trouble me often. I am inclined to think that for many psychological situations flashbacks are not straightforward. The emotion generated by one experience can be transferred to other situations if that does not sound too Freudian. I am inclined to consign most things that smack of Freud to the mental dustbin, other than his fundamental idea that behaviour has causes and we can figure them out. Freud was solidly a psychological determinist. What we do, think and feel does not just happen. There is a reason and it can be found.

I don't have flashbacks but there are social situations, or scenes in films, that make me far more uneasy than seems normal. I always think they date back to that day. I remember a girlfriend telling me over dinner that she had had a meaningless 'fling' while we were on a break, a break thought to be permanent at the time. I just could not cope with it. The memories I have of that night are, I believe, fuelled by the conversation of many years earlier, five days after that sham marriage. That girlfriend and I never got back on an even keel again, this despite the fact I had done exactly the same thing. This is not normal grown-up mature behaviour. I withdrew into my shell and even then I knew this was not the way to deal with these emotions.

I have said my positive bit about Freud, but let's not get carried away. Psychoanalysis is, in my book, a self-indulgent unscientific waste of time. It is caught well in *The Kaminsky Method* (Netflix) when Sandy (Michael Douglas) asks Mindy's twice-her-age boyfriend whether he has ever been in analysis.

For twenty years now, is the reply.

And how are you getting on, Sandy asks.

I am making good progress.

Enough said and far too close to the truth.

Then there are the nightmares and I have a gold medal in nightmares. But are they PTSD, or just nightmares which are the result of the anxieties everyone has to deal with?

There is also talk about enduring personality changes but I would not be the best person to comment on that. I am still inclined to see the best and worst in people. I still prefer to trust rather than distrust, but if I am let down I will never let it go. Anyone who knows me will tell you there are a few names that are guaranteed to spark a ten minute rant. I never learned to forgive and forget. But maybe I was always like that.

Would I have been able to have a monogamous committed intimate relationship if that betrayal had not happened? My jury is out.

Depression is a symptom, but, without making too light of it, these days everyone seems to have depression and get their fifteen minutes of media attention. Thankfully the black dog that visited Churchill has never visited me. When I hear someone like Alistair Campbell talk of his days of just not being able to face the world I know he is describing a beast I have not encountered.

There is another way of feeling that may be a result of serious shock, and that is living in the medium wave band. It is not difficult to live in a world without highs and lows and just go from day to day doing what is on the list. It is a very safe place. I did that for years. If I had won the Lotto I would have said grand and I don't know if I would have been particularly bothered if the car had been stolen. There were years of a whatever world, long before the word became commonplace when listening to disdainful teenagers. I don't really care is a very effective protective shield.

Trouble concentrating is a symptom and back in those days I learned the unfortunate skill of reading while thinking about something else. It is a plague when all of a sudden you realise you cannot remember a thing about the pages you have just turned because your mind was elsewhere and the words were just words. There were long times of just going through the motions and not really caring. About anything. It is a curse.

PTSD symptom lists talk about alcohol abuse and any of my friends will tell you there were times when I have let loose more often than I should. But I have a strong work ethic which means any such tendency is kept under control. Most of the unguarded things I have said, and regretted, have been as a result of drink being taken. But I find it difficult to think of many among my acquaintances who have not been equally guilty. When the results of the DNA test, and the news that people knew but did not tell me, came through, wine was my drug of choice to deal with the anger. It was probably only over the course of months but there were several nights when I sat alone ruminating and drank until I fell asleep. And that is forty-plus years after the event. It is easy to get into the habit of endlessly living in the past. It is easy to recall bad things, disappointments rather than the positive. If you weren't already feeling bad, you can take yourself to a darker place. This is Cognitive Behaviour Therapy. In reverse.

There was really only one symptom I looked at and said, yes, that's me alright. One of the questions you are asked is do you feel detached from other people, or somewhat estranged? Absolutely. Completely. Regularly, but not continuously. If no man is an island, I have made a good effort at being one over the years.

If you read the DSM it will tell you the best hope for full recovery is a combination of medicine and therapy. Popping a daily pill is not on my agenda. If recreational drugs were legal and quality controlled I would be all for some experimenting. However at this stage of life I do not wish to provide the embarrassment of going haywire, or dying, because of some batch of bad drugs provided by some unscrupulous criminal. That is not how I wish to be remembered. Having had a mother who was a nurse and who would have only dispensed an aspirin if your leg was hanging off, the notion of a pill cure is foreign to me. Like many psychology students I did some experimenting by faking pre-exam anxieties and going to the college psychiatrist and getting prescribed some mild tranquilizer or antidepressant ... Librium and Nardil, I recall. I never felt better. I don't deny medication may suit others. I do understand it as a part of a programme of intervention that will help people change. But I have never felt it was for me.

So to therapy? But why? Is there actually anything wrong with me? Therapy would turn off the chorus of people telling me to talk to someone and deal with the past. Does it matter if I spend a lot of my remaining time, which I hope is not short, idly staring at the mountains or the sea and watching the world go by? I am not doing any harm. And it is not as if I can refocus, get my head together, and go off and win the Nobel Prize.

Would it be better to leave the stone in my shoe? Perhaps it has become a friendly pebble.

I do. I think. I feel. I am.

THERAPY

Therapy requires a great deal of trust to allow oneself to be that vulnerable. Plus you need to believe the person who is listening can actually understand and have workable answers, that there might be a plan to get from A to B. That is a big ask when you are dealing with emotional matters where we all feel we know more than we do. It is not like going to the cancer specialist or heart surgeon, or even car mechanic, where we are quite happy to acknowledge their expertise and place ourselves in their hands. I have the boxed set of *In Treatment* and Gabriel Byrne's beautifully written and performed character was as messed up as the rest of us. I was interested to see Ryan Tubridy in an interview recently say he had once done a few counselling sessions and didn't take to it. He said he could never get out of chat show guest mode and I know exactly how he felt. I too would see it as a performance. I am too much the psychologist and I could see myself thinking a question was good or bad, predictable or unpredictable. I might have to stop myself giving them a pat on the back. Nice open question there. Good one. Plus I could imagine my father being appalled that I would discuss these things in such a setting. There was a bit of Jeremy Clarkson about my father. He was hard on himself and I have often been accused of the same.

Words come easily to me, too easily, so that they may not be connected to sufficiently honest thought or emotion. For someone who is good with words it is tempting to be too clever by half. It works both ways. A clever therapist can frame a person's experiences to see the world in a particular way that may be much more in tune with the therapist's beliefs than the client's needs. Likewise a clever client can pull the wool over the average therapist with a few half-truths. I suspect that would become my primary goal. I would be their star client, their greatest challenge. If they didn't look forward to the sessions I was not doing my part. With that mindset progress would be unlikely.

Therapy has a far greater chance of success if the goals are clear. We have all seen people who have changed behaviour with the assistance of some form of therapy, whether to quit smoking or lose weight. There is ample evidence that people can reduce their level of anxiety, improve self-confidence, learn to speak in front of a crowd, be more positive, look forward instead of living in the past. There is a great deal of research supporting the effectiveness of techniques like Cognitive Behaviour Therapy to help people think and behave in more effective ways. There is also an enormous amount of claptrap written about the power of positive thinking and counselling. Who knows how many people are being counselled weekly without any measurement of the effects?

Undoubtedly some of my attitudes, even prejudices, about talk therapies go back to my college days. I was firmly in the B.F. Skinner behaviourist camp. We wanted to make psychology more scientific, more accountable, and to measure behaviour and behaviour change. Many of those ideas are now commonplace but back then they were fiercely resisted. If behaviour was predictable then where was free will? B.F. Skinner, who was a recipient of the National Medal of Science in America in 1968, was a hero. They say you should never meet your heroes but I did and liked him and knew I was in the presence of a big mind. I interviewed him twice, once in his office in Harvard and once in his daughter's back garden in London. He stayed on message each time and some of his answers were like paragraphs from his books. There was a slight feeling of tetchiness about him … a sort of why do I have to state the obvious yet again. I didn't even get a photo with him, but he did sign my well-thumbed copy of *Beyond Freedom and Dignity*. As an aside, this same daughter had been the subject of dreadful rumours because he had carried out some applied behaviour analysis in her upbringing and published the results. The word was that she was institutionalised, which shows fake news and conspiracy theories have been around for a while. For the record she was perfectly normal and made us cups of tea on a sunny summer afternoon.

In the other psychological corner was Carl Rogers. He was highly influential as talking therapies and counselling were developed. Much of what Freud and Jung had written had been largely discounted by then, some half a century ago. We learned about it as one would learn history. That some people still take psychoanalysis seriously today amuses, even appals, me.

Rogers was the recipient of many prestigious awards and possibly would have been proudest of Humanist of the Year in 1964. In a survey in 1982 he was considered the most influential psychotherapist in history. His book *Client-Centred Therapy* was the alternative Bible for many students. His brand of non-directive therapy held that the solution was within the person and it was the therapist's job to allow or assist it to emerge. This was anathema to me as a student, though I have softened. That form of therapy has become a great deal more structured over the years. I was fortunate to also interview Rogers when he was in Dublin for a conference. Again, I liked the man. During the interview he conceded that non-directive was an aim and one he did not always accomplish. I have been contacted by a few people over the years who tell me this is one of the very few times he said something like this. Again I didn't get a selfie but I do have a copy of *On Becoming a Person* which he signed. Again, I knew I was in the presence of a big mind, but a word of caution. Despite his lifetime study of the mind and behaviour, and eminence as a psychotherapist, he admitted having his own difficulties and for many years consumed a bottle of vodka daily.

It is probably well-nigh impossible to be with a therapist who has not been influenced by one, or both, of these giants. They may not be aware of it but, just as Rock 'n Roll goes back to the Blues and Chuck Berry, modern psychology was shaped by the work of these people. But what modern therapy was it that I wanted, or needed? If I cannot even specify it clearly we are not off to a good start. Is change even the goal? Perhaps it is just to understand, believing that such insight will bring the desired change in its wake. It seems a little perverse to sit down opposite a trained professional psychologist and say, I don't really know why I am here but I had a bad experience fifty years ago and my friends tell me I never got over it. Fix me please. It feels too much like being a hippie in a tie-dyed T shirt talking about going to India to find myself. I know how my father would have reacted to that once he had stopped laughing. Perhaps he was an overly practical person.

My psychological warts are part of me. They give me an excuse for some self-pity on a bad day. They give me explanations for some of the quirks in my make-up that I grandiosely refer to as personality. Why go to therapy? If those quirks get smoothed out then I would stop being me. I would probably become a blander me rather than a more effective creative version. I have no desire to walk around with a self-satisfied grin. If I travel inside my skull I don't want to be bored. Therapy may be a step more humane than lobotomy, but is the target not the same? I still felt uneasy about the idea and gradually the notion grew in my head of writing about the events as a way of dealing with them. Perhaps writing them down honestly would work. Could it be that easy? No. It wouldn't be easy but nothing worthwhile ever is.

The day after I wrote the previous page, I found several mentions of PTSD in the Sunday newspapers. It seems to be very easy for anyone who has had issues, and is doing a confessional interview to promote something or other, to reach into the PTSD catch-all box. I remember from my days as a psychology student being taught to be wary of something which appears to explain everything. It probably explains very little when dealing with our mental and emotional worlds. We may be predictable animals if we know the correct information to enable prediction. Any computer scientist who writes the algorithms for Facebook could tell you how predictable we all are. But we remain far from simple. Self-analysis is a very inexact science, and few of us see ourselves as other see us.

Know thyself was one of three maxims written on the Temple of Apollo at Delphi, so it has been around as a psychological problem for millennia and seen as something of a conundrum from the earliest of times. People have not changed fundamentally in the last few thousand years. Stephen Hawking described us as an advanced breed of monkeys who can understand the Universe. We are social animals who laugh, cry, tell stories, like to be liked. People use and abuse power, tell the truth and tell lies, and a lot in between. None of us lead exemplary lives. At various points in life we all spend some time wondering how we became what we are. Who is this person I am and how did I become that person? Driving this self-examination is the need for something to change and for life to improve. A happy person is not going to waste too many hours examining how this pleasant fate befell them. There is a huge difference between seeking ways to make what is good better, which most of us do, and exploring ways which might result in making something bad better, which many of us postpone, or avoid. If there was an Olympic sport for denial or procrastination this field would be crowded and I think I would be in the medals.

This self-reflection is a well-meaning, if somewhat narcissistic, exercise. It is something of a personal experiment. I am not writing an autobiography, or even a memoir. It is more of a psycho-biography. Much of our behaviour and inner life is not logical. But it is in some way psycho-logical. It is not random. Nothing happens by chance. We just don't know the cause. When looking at behaviour we try to recall the things that have had a lasting emotional effect on us. None of us is an island so what changes one person inevitably has a knock on effect on other people and this may not be for the better. The people who have told me I need to deal with this deserve the courtesy of an attempt. So it seemed obvious to begin with the biggest elephant in my particular room, those four words in a bedroom more than a generation ago.

Our emotional lives are complex. I have seen people distraught by what would appear to be the most trivial of slights. There are things that made us cry or laugh, remarks that made us feel small, and resentful, social situations where we feel we belong and times when we feel like an outsider and wish the ground would swallow us. We all have achievements of which we are proud, and probably behaviour of which we are ashamed. We all have a public life, a private life and a secret life. In times of trouble we have experienced hope, and despair. Yes, there are breaches of trust, or thoughtlessness, but we also come across people whose kindness and thoughtfulness go above and beyond what was normal. Just what was the recipe that made me 'me' and you 'you' and is there much any of us can do about it if we come to the conclusion that some of the ingredients in our particular recipe are not the best?

Incidentally the other two Delphic maxims on the outside of the Temple of Apollo were *Nothing to excess* which is probably good advice though it sounds a little dull, and *Surety brings ruin* which is a touch out of date. Surety was to pledge one's actual self to secure a debt so if you did not pay you became a slave. Even the banks don't quite ask for that.

As an earlier version of neither a borrower nor a lender be it is sage advice. There were 147 maxims in all and if you strip away some that do not apply to today's society (*Control your wife*, for example) there is one hell of a lot of good advice there and as a guide for how to live they are a lot more useful than the Ten Commandments. As it happens they were around a few hundred years earlier.

A therapist would most likely, by now, have gently coaxed me back to the central point. They would have spotted my ability to move on from dealing with my scar tissue by demonstrating just how little effect it all had on me. They would have seen me scarper into the safe emotion-free world of the intellect. They would have noted I seemed reluctant to examine the hurts, and joys of my earlier life, that I would always prefer to think than feel. They might also have realised that the nineteen-year-old me was already full of anger, resentment and outrage at perceived slights and injustices. I was once a teenager who felt I would go somewhere, that I would make a mark. That night, when I was told the truth, my dreams dimmed. Reality kicked in far too early in my life. I had screwed up and in my psychological make-up that meant I would be punished by life for life.

The real surprise I got while delving into my past was that, while I tried to focus on the events surrounding the deception, my mind kept drifting back further to my days in secondary school. Walking down the aisle I took the rap for something I didn't do. But just as fresh in my mind was an incident that happened in the classroom when I was thirteen. It brings with it a lasting sense of being wronged despite being, on the face of it, quite trivial.

I was in Form 3A. My pencil dropped off the desk and I bent down to pick it up to hear, Masterson, see me after class. I did some mild protesting until the guy I shared the desk with told me to shut up because the female teacher had thought I was looking up her skirt. I cannot remember my punishment. It was probably something mindless like lines. But I can clearly remember being one hundred per cent innocent and resenting the injustice of it, just as much then as I do today! Today I am as angry about that injustice as the day it happened. No matter what I said, I was not believed and not being believed when telling the truth leaves a deep mark.

SCHOOL

Just how well do any of us understand ourselves? While we inevitably change over the years, we do not lose that feeling of being one person from early consciousness, perhaps even pre-school, to later life. When I try to understand why I do, or feel, something, I find my memory drifting towards events that have emotion as a big component. These events and emotions feel like the engine that drives me, or perhaps the triggers that fire the engine. And when they don't fire me up they put the brakes on. It may be these small scenarios that are peculiar to us, that form the foundation of the different personalities, and problems, we all have.

I am five and a half and it is my first day at school. I have four biros of different colours and am very proud of them. Another parent makes a remark to my mother along the lines of my being spoiled … maybe thinking I was better than the other children. It was negative and I still feel on the defensive as I recall it. It was a remark made out of jealousy by an adult. Despite learning later in life that this type of spiteful remark was typical of that person, I carry the emotion with me today.

It is Saturday night. I am fifteen. Tomorrow is Long Sunday. We are allowed out for the full day. It keeps me going. A few of us are chatting in dorm. We are excited about tomorrow. There is a creak on the stairs. We freeze. Sure enough he opens the door and he shines a torch around. We all pretend to be asleep. He leaves. We wait and breathe a sigh of relief as we hear him go down the stairs and close the corridor door. We wait a few minutes and began to chat again. He opens the door immediately with his Gotcha excitement and demands to know who was talking. A few of us own up and have our leave stopped immediately. But my parents will be here at nine, I protest. You should have thought of that, Masterson, before talking after lights out, I am told.

They arrived in the morning, after the two hour drive from Kilkenny to Dublin, to be told they could not see me because of my behaviour. They were sensible people and by then they could see who was the problem. Until her dying day my mother often spoke of the vindictiveness of that teacher for whom she had no respect. I spent that full term permanently gated, which almost became a badge of honour. Thankfully it would not be allowed to happen today. No parent would tolerate it.

I am in third class. I have a question to ask the teacher. I put up my hand. He beckons to me. My voice breaks as I speak. I don't speak. I squawk. Sorry, what was that question again from the corncrake?

I still feel the embarrassment today as I write this down. I was already known as a bit of a smart Alec and the teacher didn't miss the opportunity to put me down. I don't think the teacher meant any harm, though in retrospect he did turn out to be something of a bully at sports training. His one sentence ensured I kept my mouth shut for a long time. I also left the school choir in which I enjoyed singing, and didn't sing again until in my fifties when I rediscovered the pleasure it gives, a pleasure I had missed all those years since family sing-songs in the evening or in the car with us belting out *Seven little girls sitting in the back seat, kissing and a hugging with Fred.*

Some fifteen years later, when I was teaching in Trinity College, one of the class had a name I had not heard before. I gently ridiculed it and got a laugh. Immediately my corncrake moment came into my mind and I apologised. I still feel shame at what I did, though in the grand scheme of things it does not seem like much of an offence. It was with some relief that years later I saw in a newspaper that the student was making quite a success of their life. I was tempted to get in touch and apologise again, but all I would have been doing was looking for absolution. What was done was done, and hopefully it never crossed their mind again. They probably had a more robust self-concept than I had. Power comes in many forms and insecurity can make it very easy to abuse.

Over the years I have often been a vocal supporter of boarding school, despite hating most of the moments I spent in one. Six of my most formative years, from eleven to seventeen, were spent in that institution in Dublin where I most certainly did not belong, and for which I still feel resentment. If I was asked which would I change if I could live my life over again, my boarding school days or the deception I suffered as a young adult, it would be a toss-up. If that school made me feel like an outsider then the betrayal was the icing on the cake.

I recently read Louis de Bernières', author of *Captain Corelli's Mandolin* among other fine books, reflections on his boarding school days which were horrendously abusive, both physically and sexually. He felt unable to write about them until both of his parents were dead as he acknowledges they believed they were doing what was best for him and did not appreciate the brutality that went with it. It was to make him self-sufficient, so self-sufficient he observed as to never be able to make a relationship last. That observation stopped me in my tracks. I used to think self-sufficiency was a totally positive thing. No more. When faced with trauma as a nineteen-year-old, my self-sufficiency sustained me, but it also became a cage from which there was no escape.

Thankfully, unlike de Bernières or John Boyne or Brian D'Arcy, sexual and physical abuse were entirely absent in the school where I spent six years. There were however many teachers who had swallowed enough religion to enable them to justify their petty psychological cruelties towards anyone who did not share their outlook. It gave me a healthy fear of religion and to this day I remain very cautious about people who are too sure they have God on their side. Born Again Americans terrify me. One century it is the Crusades. Another it is the Twin Towers and beheadings. But always there are the foot soldiers with their childish certainties. During my schooldays some of them seemed to specialise in making my life a misery.

As a child of Protestant, but not particularly religious, parents in rural Ireland, education posed a problem. There was no non-Catholic secondary school that taught to Leaving Cert level in Kilkenny. Even at that age both my parents would have wanted me to have the university education they were not lucky enough to receive. There was no family business to inherit so I would be making my own way. My father maintained a lifelong resentment towards his own father, primarily because my grandfather refused to pay for my father to go to third level.

His main reason appeared to be that he himself had left school at fifteen. My father was not going to allow that to happen again.

I had the benefit of a two-teacher primary school education in Kilkenny where both teachers saw their job as making sure every child, whatever their abilities, did as well as they could. It was the best start any child could have wished for, an atmosphere of security and challenge as every school should be, but sadly many are not. When I was ten it was decided I should sit the scholarship exam to go to school in Dublin. I was sat in a room supervised for three hours by Rev Harold Good, the same man who later oversaw the IRA decommissioning of weapons. He made sure I didn't cheat. I am not sure if he was as fortunate with the IRA. I won the scholarship and my future was decided in those few hours. I was to receive free education in a boarding school in the capital for the next six years. My parents would have been able to pay but it would have meant sacrifices and every little helped. The article in the local paper headed *First in Fifty* was the first time I remember my name in the paper, though I had won several pen sets, a matching fountain pen, biro and propelling pencil in a case, in the *Sunday Independent* competitions that I loved, and it must have been there also. Seeing my name in print made me feel real. Years later, it is a feeling I have never entirely lost.

Two things dominate my memory of secondary school. Firstly that institution was far too conservative for me, and secondly I hated being away from home. Homesickness was ever present for the next year. My parents eventually offered to let me come home but I was used to it by then and said I would stick it out. While thinking about this recently it surprised me how few happy memories I have of the next six years. I was troublesome. No doubt about it. I had a great time as a twelve-year-old asking the teacher to prove it in religion classes. There was a good science lab so it was only reasonable to apply scientific method more widely. Teachers do not like having their faith questioned by children, but I got great satisfaction from annoying them. Eventually there was an edict banning the phrase *prove it*. I think it is not uncommon for questioning children to have a rough time with some teachers as mediocre teachers resent being shown up by clever youngsters.

There were occasional positives. The school was co-educational. I credit that normality as the reason why I have always enjoyed the company of women as friends. And secondly there were some excellent teachers. Many people are lucky to meet an inspirational teacher and I was lucky to have had three.

There was a French teacher who made a point of singling me out in front of the class and acknowledging that I had got a bad press but she had put it out of her mind and was delighted to compliment me on my work and results. I was fourteen and that still brings tears to my eyes. She was a young woman with a mind of her own who, sadly for the pupils, soon left to begin a family. Thank you Miss Johnston. You had no idea how much that meant.

We had a Chemistry teacher who took an interest in a group of us that he knew were inquisitive. He made us think, answered our questions, was well able to say I don't know which is an important thing to teach. I have been interested in science ever since. Thank you Dick O'Connor. There are a few of us who never meet without recalling what you did for us.

And there was a music teacher who always took time to play music that he thought I should hear. *Rhapsody in Blue* was a favourite. He used to say, 'George Gershwin is dead but I don't have to believe it if I don't want to.' Gershwin was only thirty-eight when he died and I believe the comment was first made by a well-known American short story writer and columnist, John O'Hara.

Another favourite was Ravel's *Bolero*. He was also one of the first people in authority in my life to say out loud that he thought the Beatles were here to stay and weren't just a long-haired fad as was the received wisdom of the day. He regularly played their songs and commented on the quality of the melody. Thank you Frank Hughes. Your kindness and imagination still pop into my mind often. Those three people could think for themselves. They encouraged curiosity and learning and they saved me. I still wish I had met them elsewhere.

I have one other truly happy memory. The very pious teacher who was responsible for the sneaky raid on our dormitory had a parrot of which he was very proud. All of us passed it on our way to breakfast. The bird had a good ear and after a week of every young boy saying fuck off to it we got the desired result. Sadly the unfortunate bird's freedom was as curtailed as mine when he began to perform. He was never seen in public again. I still feel not the tiniest regret for this incident. That teacher had it coming.

PARENTS

Many years later, at a graduate art exhibition in Glasgow, I bought a poster which read *I kind of have a dream*. I hung it in my study. At the time I just thought it was a clever idea. It was there a long time before I realised it described my plight since that long distant night. I wondered what was in the head of the young girl who made this piece of art as a final year project and was probably glad to make a sale. Had something happened to dull her ambition? Was she just pleasantly ironic? To really excel you need to put your head above the parapet. You draw attention to yourself. Most of me wanted to hide. I was terrified to walk across the open square at the front of Trinity College. I would have felt that people would look at me and maybe talk about me and it would not be good. I scurried around the edges invisibly for years.

I lost all purpose in life except perhaps to make amends to my parents in some way. I may not have ruined my life but I felt sure I ruined theirs. I stayed in TCD when I probably should have emigrated. That is not to say I did not enjoy my time at TCD. I loved it but, looked at from today's perspective, staying in Ireland was not a good decision. It barely deserves to be called a decision at all. Few of the people I was friendly with and were of similar ability to me stayed in Ireland. It was not a land of opportunity. America, Canada, and Australia were the magnets and I am still in touch with people who never for an instant regretted leaving this island. I got my PhD which made my mother and father proud, but they never forgot the events of a few years before. I think they saw it as further proof that, despite being given all the opportunities, I had made a horrendous mess of my life and that saddened them.

When I became a lecturer in TCD they were again proud, though by then perhaps a bit mystified. The proper time for me to move back to TCD would have been in my forties or fifties after a lot of experience in universities abroad. What I did was too much like the unadventurous teacher who goes back to the school they left a few years before to join the staff, with little new to bring with them.

I loved that teaching job. But it just happened to me. It was not an ambition fulfilled. I was by then drifting and felt a bit of a fraud. I felt I didn't deserve good things. Punishment would have been more understandable. Life was happening to me. I wasn't making it happen. I didn't seem to have to try hard. To become a lecturer in an institution I hugely admired should have been a source of pride. Instead I felt that after what had happened I did not deserve this chance. That said, the work ethic I learned at home kicked in. Somehow I grasped it with both hands. If I got really stuck in I could come to deserve it, and I lived, breathed and ate that job. Probably for the first time since primary school I began to feel I might be where I belonged. On the outside I was happy.

I had done nineteen years of living before being conned into walking up the aisle. It wasn't like my life began that day, or indeed the day I was told the truth. A different person would not have had the same sense of responsibility. A different person would have smelt a rat. Looking back it seems I was book-clever, strong-minded and street-stupid. I still am. I am genuinely shocked to this day when someone tells me a lie to my face. It is as if I learned nothing. I am fundamentally the same person as I was back then.

By any criteria I had a supportive upbringing from caring parents who enjoyed a good marriage and wanted the best for me. Their good marriage, as much as the betrayal of trust I experienced, may have laid the foundation for what I expected from an intimate relationship. The bar was set impossibly high from the start. A woman friend with similarly happy parents told me she recognised those feelings. We both recalled with fondness waking and hearing our parents still chatting into the night.

Before I went to boarding school I suspect I was as happy as any child is lucky enough to be. I know I was able to tell the time on my first day at school. I can recall sitting on my father's knee as he used the alarm clock to teach me and test me. I am certain I was given enthusiastic encouragement. I was probably paraded in front of people who dropped in to the house and had to endure me performing my John telling the time party trick. It did have two lasting effects. From that early age I was very comfortable with numbers and could manipulate them easily in my head. Numeracy is fundamental to modern day life and I am glad I got it early. I find it hard to understand how people cannot instantly calculate a percentage. Every now and again I hear some figures on the radio or TV and intuitively react with that doesn't add up, while others in my company have let it go by without batting an eyelid. I believe Paul McCartney finds it hard to understand that everyone cannot just sit down at a piano and come up with a song. Would that I had his gift and not mine.

My father hated fishing but he spent hours on the river bank with me because I went through a phase of loving it. As a teenager my mother drove myself and friends all over the place to compete in golf competitions. Life was good.

Another lesson I learned in those early days has been more of a monkey on my back. I learned that you have to do or achieve something to get praise and respect. It has to be earned. Effort matters. Just existing is a cop out. The Protestant work ethic is a real sociological construct, though it has little to do with Protestantism. This upbringing was the polar opposite of the cotton wool kids of today who are praised to the heights for any attempt they make. Many are shielded from feelings of failure and, as a result, are very unprepared for the vicissitudes of the real world. I would have understood that failure is an option, but lack of effort was not. What one had to do to avoid failure was to work hard. That work ethic was a given. Fortunately I did not encounter many failures in large chunks of life but, that said, any time I did is seared into my mind. I still recall the absolute horror when I failed my first motorbike test for not doing enough lifesavers (bikers will know this involves looking over your shoulder and not relying on your mirrors). It was a good lesson, but I felt so ashamed that I had got into the habit of looking at wing mirrors and not double-checking. I was mortified when I had to tell a few fellow bikers. Gay Byrne, wearing his Road Safety Authority hat, was delighted that the system worked!

When we think about how we became what we are, we go to the obvious genetic hand we are dealt as well as our experiences through life.

Despite having had very caring parents I often hear Philip Larkin's poem from the sixties about how your parents fuck you up in my head. It is not that they mean to but the nature of life is you inherit all their faults with a few extra added just for you.

I always take those lines to mean that you are dealt an individual genetic hand and that hand will have a big impact on your future. There are things that happen in life that cannot be reversed no matter how much one might wish it. It may be the person who drank too much before driving and the following crash may have changed many lives. It may be a remark spoken in anger that cannot be unsaid.

We are all influenced by people and events, but it has often struck me that there are probably only fifty or a hundred things, leaving aside genetics (which is a big leaving aside), that have a major impact on the sort of person or personality we become. It is a touch unsettling to realise how much of what we do is on automatic pilot. Even our conversations are often so predictable that we do not need to engage our thought processes. We can rabbit on for ages. How often do we stop and say, 'I need to think about that'? Typically we just keep on talking to fill the silences with as much skill and as little thought as a boxer who moves to avoid a punch. Many of our routine utterances are out of our mouth before even a millisecond of thought is applied. Compare that behaviour with how slowly we talk when we have to actually consider what our words mean and what effect they might have. It is an easy way to help you realise that talking often requires little or no thought.

"That's not like you."

That is what people say when you do something out of character. You might agree or disagree. But you will be in no doubt that you are you. You might even agree with the person that it wasn't typical of your behaviour, without doubting the you who did something is the same you that has a cup of coffee first thing each morning. You are the same you whether you helped a stranger, told a lie, slept with your wife's best friend, or gave a chunk of money to a charity. You may be very complex in the choices you are able to make and the life you lead. Or you may live a life of predictable dullness. But through your years on this planet it is the same you that feels the pleasure and the pain, the energy and the lethargy, the love and the hate, the mania and the depression, the hope and the desperation, the ecstasy and the despair. That you is a person with personality, abilities and beliefs who usually does not have a very good idea of who they are or how they came to be that way.

When you are getting to know someone, you tell each other stories. It is the way you display what sort of person you are, or more accurately, how you wish to be seen. Typically you are looking for overlaps in your interests and views that are conducive to spending time together that will be enjoyable. You may not be one hundred per cent honest but that, in itself, tells you a bit about yourself. I can recall with horror a few occasions when I pretended to know something I did not know. I fondly think, or delude myself, that I was not found out. Two of those occasions just stung into my mind, despite the fact they were inconsequential and happened over thirty years ago. In one I pretended to know something about soccer that I did not know. I was just trying to be part of the conversation. And in the other it was about music and I was trying to impress. I still cringe as I think of them now. Relatively small things can have a substantial long-lasting effect. But both examples illustrate to me that I am, by and large, truthful. Looking at his public utterances one can safely assume Donald Trump is not troubled by such memories.

There may well be things of which you are not overly proud and they will be edited or deleted. Other stories will get more emphasis than they might deserve. Much of what makes you the person you are resides in your secret life. It is there in your memory as a story, one that you can at least tell yourself. My hunch is that it is far easier to identify the changes in another person with whom one is involved that it is to do so looking at oneself. Just how well do any of us understand ourselves?

Have I remained oversensitive? Certainly not in work situations where most things I have worked on involve a lot of smart people who express opinions. They are intended to improve the work. Having gone through philosophy tutorials, which were exercises in ripping each other's arguments apart, someone telling me to edit here rather than there does not bother me. A personal criticism (you sounded full of yourself at the meeting / you were very rude to Joan / I was embarrassed by what you said in front of Peter) can, by contrast, keep me awake and ruminating for nights.

Some early things stick and I have to remind myself that I did not become a different person the night I was told the baby was not mine.

There was already a lot of me hard-wired and a lot of me formed by learnings that were brought to that situation.

We like to think of ourselves beginning life as a blank slate, a tabula rasa, that has infinite possibilities. Obviously, despite an entire industry of motivational quotes, that isn't the case. At 5 foot 8 and a half I wasn't ever going to be a basketball pro, and coming from Kilkenny the chances of becoming an astronaut were slim. There is not a lot we can do with the genetic hand we are dealt, bits of each of our parents placing boundaries on our possibilities. It is that genetic soup that interacts with the world and makes us what we are.

Undoubtedly our experiences change us, or, more properly, what we make of those experiences and how or whether they affect us. How soon many of the building blocks of our personality are in place is a moot point. I went to a school reunion some twenty years after the Leaving Certificate and met many people whom I had not seen in the interim. There were no surprises. Poodles had not turned into Alsatians. By and large the gregarious people were still gregarious and the shy ones still shy. Some accents had changed, but only slightly. People were just somewhat older versions of themselves as I had remembered them. There were no shocks, or, sadly, surprises. Many had physical mannerisms that had not changed and were instantly recognisable. I can see many in myself that are identical to my father. I did not copy him. They must be wired in. Bono has written about hearing his father's voice in him when he sings. I think all men have that experience in middle age and it is quite troubling for our sense of uniqueness.

Mindset is a good word. We do get set in our behaviours, but also in our thoughts. Most of us live in a daily, weekly and annual structure so that we can do things without the inconvenience of making a decision. Likewise we get set in the mental and emotional ways that we approach things. A new experience provokes anxiety in one person and excitement in another. Each of those is a heightened state of arousal which tells us a lot more about our personality than routine existence.

It is not the bigger events – the births, marriages, engagements, deaths, the social announcement column events – that make us different. They are merely milestones we project to the world. To understand oneself involves looking at the smaller things, good and bad, and spotting patterns and habits that make us what we are.

The clock cannot be turned back and no matter how much I might have wanted to make it up to my parents I could never change the fundamental fact that I had let them down. Yes, things happened that they were proud of. I have a photo on my fridge of them standing either side of me in TCD when I was awarded my PhD and looking overdressed in the red and gold gown. But I know my mother would have happily swapped that for a photo in which I had a happy wife, and maybe the prospect of grandchildren. My mother was impressed by my working in RTE and would have been delighted to see me produce *The Late Late Show*, but sadly she did not live to see that. There wasn't anything I did, or could have done, that would have made up for the time she spent watching a teenage girl go through a pregnancy she believed was the result of her son's stupidity. As guilt trips go it was a fairly big one.

I think it is fair to say that people from a Protestant background in the Republic of Ireland always feel something of the outsider. Growing up in provincial Ireland as part of the loosely knit Protestant community, it was clear we had a lot more in common with Southern Catholics than with Northern Protestants who may as well have been from a different planet. We were Irish. Yet it was not uncommon for me to meet someone, when playing in golf competitions, who had never met a Protestant before. It would come up in conversation if I said where I went to school. And the mostly, though not always, unspoken sentiment was that I somehow wasn't fully Irish. There was also a suggestion that we thought of ourselves as that bit better and that there was no such thing as a poor Protestant, both of which were untrue. There were odd times when I would hear conversations about how ridiculous it was for Catholics to believe in transubstantiation, when the speaker was quite at home with the virgin birth or the equally unbelievable resurrection. When such nonsense abounded it was easy to be an atheist from an early age.

My parents were not snobs. But they belonged to a different tribe from most of the people we met. They had that post-independence determination to be normal, not to stand out. They had a strong helping of keep your head down and don't draw attention to yourself. I remember saying to my father during the early IRA campaigns that there was no possibility of any of us in the South being targeted. He was cautious. I remember him saying, It only takes one headbanger.

They were Protestant in a cultural way but I doubt that, if put to the pin of their collar, they had much belief in a God or any at all in an afterlife. We were not a grace before meals family. My mother religiously saluted magpies. She was of that Ireland that didn't have the confidence to ask for red or white, and would have thought it wasteful not to make a lamp out of an empty Mateus Rosé bottle. If there were ever prayers before bedtime it stopped when I was six or seven. That said, I do remember them having a routine of going to church every morning at eight during Lent. I think that was more discipline than religion, more supporting the local community, than prayer. Their values, like those of our friends and neighbours of both and no religions, were all derived from Christianity. They were both scrupulously honest. Telling a lie would have been a major sin in their eyes.

My mother was a nurse and she would have seen the virgin birth as preposterous. As theatre sister she at times sterilised instruments for surgeons when there was no operation planned. It was unspoken, but the only use for these instruments was for a middle-class abortion. A lot of blind eyes were turned. And yet she had a somewhat fearful attitude to casual sex which went back to a scene she told me about more than once when an unfortunate prostitute was placed on a table naked in front of a group of student nurses so they could see, up close, the horrific effects of advanced venereal disease. It made a lasting impression on her. She described it very graphically to me once and I will spare your sensibilities. It was not a pleasant sight. It was enough to banish any thoughts of premarital sex and scare you into lifelong monogamy. As it happened my parents adored each other so monogamy was never an issue.

My mother was the more straightforward of my parents. She was a great deal less complicated than my father and I do not mean that in any superior or judgemental fashion. My father always resented his father for not giving him the chance to go to college. I don't think he liked his father very much for all sorts of reasons. My grandfather was a dreadfully self-centred man, so maybe that is where I got it from. I never heard Dad speak of him with any affection or admiration. My mother was very happy with her lot. Her father died when she was four and she was brought up with the assistance of The Masonic Order, of which her father was a member. My grandmother had a bachelor lodger who took a great interest in the upbringing of my mother and uncle. I have the dimmest recollection of the man known as Mr Jack. He was a good amateur painter and exhibited at the RHA and I have some of his work.

When Mr Jack died my grandmother came to live with us for the last few years of her life and she was very much part of the family. Her death when I was fifteen was my first real experience of loss and I am sure my mother was thankful she was not alive to witness the events of a few years later. My mother was always being told by us that she worried too much, but in truth she really only worried about her children. When you argued with her she always brought the subject back to basics. In the case of my girlfriend's pregnancy she always came back to if you had never gone near her there wouldn't have been any doubt. She meant it as a matter of fact, unarguable statement, but it did always feel like a stick she used to beat me. In her mind I could be as clever as I liked and do well at school and at university but somehow this simple truth had escaped me. Long before her death, which was long before the DNA test, I think she knew as well as I did that I was not the father. Yet had I presented the test to her in black and white it would not have changed a thing. Her line was simple and it was that if I had behaved differently there could not have been even the tiniest doubt and she was right. I may have wanted to scream the test result from the rooftops to her. But to what avail? Was I still looking for absolution from her? Probably.

I let my father down in an additional way that caused lasting hurt. The five or so months before Áine was born were full of confusion. Having agreed to break up after she was born, we really had no firm plans as to how to do that. It was, to say the least, a complicated situation with a baby due to be born in the Spring. Over Christmas I confided in a family friend who would have known nothing of the real situation. I suppose I needed to talk to someone but my father never forgave me for discussing family business outside the family before raising it at home. I frequently protested that I only did so because I really did not know what I was doing and that, if by any chance we had stayed together, I never wanted him and Mum to know. He never accepted that. It was a deep hurt, but mercifully one that seemed to heal when I spent a lot of time with him while my mother was dying and after. Compared to losing her after a short nine week illness nothing much mattered to him for quite a while. When he remarried two years later I was his best man.

In my night terrors I had not usually dreamed of trying to contact him. Was it because there was no need, that the healing was done? I don't think so. It was more because when it came to things that mattered it was my mother who took the lead. If I got to her she would take care of him.

A psychologist friend suggested I write to my mother to figure out what I would say to her were it possible. This is as close as I have got. And now I think of it she wouldn't care a damn about the events of years ago. She would be all questions about today and how people were. She would probably be glad about the introduction of divorce and marriage equality but she wouldn't have much interest in discussing such world-shattering events. It would be all about people. She would be sad to hear of Áine's early death and say something like, That poor girl got a very raw deal and she didn't do anything wrong. If I mentioned PTSD she might burst out laughing. She would sum up, telling me to get on with life, to stop worrying about her, and to stop being a bloody fool and enjoy every minute of life. She was very angry her own life was ending with such short notice. She felt robbed. She had a very good understanding of how the minutes all matter and would not have wanted them wasted.

That was years ago, she might say. And you were a bloody fool, but sure you know that already.

Absolution. Some chance.

Take some responsibility for being happy. Get on with it.

Ok. I hear you. Now please let me get the occasional good night's sleep. Oh and by the way, I ended up working with Gay Byrne.

Ah. I always loved Gay. I hope he put manners on you.

DAYLIGHT

I began the process of writing about the deception I encountered for three reasons.

Firstly, I knew I had to do something. For years I had masked the hurts with work and I loved work. I was fortunate to enjoy what I was doing most of the time, but work wasn't delivering the escape as effectively as it used to. When I wasn't working I was going through the motions of life and even I could see it. I was dull. Then the conversations and texts with Áine after the conclusive DNA test, and then her death, had brought it all back for a second double whammy at a point when I had more time to think. If I was going to make anything of the final quarter of my life I needed to get a grip.

Secondly, some people close to me had been telling me I needed therapy and that I had to deal with things. Apparently I was sinking. They could see me animated on the phone. They could read me writing with occasional wit and insight, and they could hear me belly laughing and performing live on the local radio. Then they would see me the rest of the time deflated, with no interest in anything, listless and a bit irritable, with no emotions either good or bad, drifting from day to day. Not surprisingly they were concerned and thought more than the batteries needed to be changed.

Thirdly, I could not reconcile myself to the notion of therapy. When the issues were based on deception, the required vulnerability of opening up to another person would not be easy. There was one skilled person I could have trusted but it would have changed the relationship from the friendship it is and I did not want that. When I was training to become a psychotherapist years back one of the requirements was that I undertook regular counselling. During those sessions I never once made reference to what had to have been the major psychological event of my life. I knew I could easily play that game ad nauseam. I decided to give it one last try and selected DIY as the method of choice. And not talking, but writing. You cannot cheat as much if the words are there looking back at you. Words matter, and they can keep you honest when they are written down.

I wrote each day with much the same amount of emotional input as I had done for years writing for the *Sunday Independent*. Very little. I did it in much the same way. I walked around thinking out roughly what I was trying to say. That is always the time-consuming part and the emotionally intense part. Then I would put the emotions to one side and sit down to write. For an article I would write a rapid first draft and leave it for a few hours, or overnight, depending on the deadline. Then go back and finish it. I did the same with this. It has never ceased to amaze me how much thinking the brain does for you while you are not even trying to think. Ideas and problems get sorted out in the background when you are out for a walk or run, or even watching television. The unconscious mind never seems to stop working. With this project it worked overtime with a vengeance.

If I ever doubted that the topics I was writing about were significant to me psychologically then the night-time made it very clear to me that I was uncovering a minefield. Night after night I awoke in terror from repetitive nightmares with an intensity I had not felt for many years. Some nights I would turn over and go straight back into the mental hell. Others I lay awake, waiting for the dawn and terrified to relax or close my eyes. I would listen to Radio 4 to distract me and, after the *Today* show headlines at 6am, I might drift off peacefully for an hour. Was this doing me any good? Was such turmoil to be expected? I had no idea. I don't tend to have much time for the various hydraulic metaphors for mental life. I grimace when I hear of dams bursting and feelings pouring out and relieving the pressure. I have never had much time for any of the party trick psychobabble about what dreams are supposed to mean. Whatever was happening certainly wasn't making me feel any better, but I persisted in writing thoughts down and gradually the nightmares waned.

My daytime was normal. I continued going through the motions of living without much life in me. I made lists and ticked off tasks as they were completed. In between I spent hours staring at the view in front of me. And then one Tuesday I felt different. I felt good. There was a spring in my step that had been absent for longer than I care to remember. I had almost totally forgotten the feeling.

Had I been depressed? People who knew me had told me I had. If that is the case I spent much of my adult life depressed. When people talk about depression it is not something I recognise in myself. As I said earlier I have never had a day when I could not get out of bed. I have never not completed a task. I never avoided work, or socialising. But in many aspects of my life I had been acting for a long time. I did not feel anything, so I just behaved as if I had the feelings I knew or thought were appropriate. There were no highs or lows. Just a permanent medium. There was very little I actually looked forward to.

That Tuesday morning the first sign was physical. I felt strong. I was walking with purpose. I wasn't just going from A to B. There was purpose. I was looking ahead. Once you pass the age of sixty it becomes easier to think of tiredness as normal. You can explain things away as part of the ageing process, even when they aren't. That morning I got up, had a shower, got dressed and the clock turned back years. I felt refreshed. And then it struck me again. I hadn't felt this good in a long time.

I don't remember joy, but that Tuesday morning I felt that it was again possible. The feeling didn't last long, but now I knew it was there somewhere and whatever self-examination I was doing was not a total self-indulgent waste of time. Looking back it occurred to me I hadn't done anything wrong. An outsider might say I behaved well and with some moral fibre. It wasn't my fault, so why had I beaten myself up for decades, and hurt a few innocent victims along the way who were unfortunate enough to fall in love with me for a while.

Just maybe there is more to PTSD than I had given it credit for. And possibly depression doesn't have to be the full black dog. It is difficult to write about either these days without appearing to be desperately needy and in search of a fifteen minute fix of fame.

I began having a new recurring dream. I am with a woman who is not anyone I know, or knew, and indeed I cannot bring a face to my memory now. She is blond, speaks softly, has blue eyes and soft skin. There is a feeling of love and trust and warmth. There is a total connection. It is a non-sexual situation, just more like arms around each other and looking into each other's eyes. After a short time of the intimacy I withdraw and just keep on telling her I can't … I can't and wake up.

I know I felt the love. Maybe I also felt the vulnerability and that was enough to bring the shutters down. There was no face, no accent, but the general features were somewhat reminiscent of those of my childhood sweetheart. I began to feel I was looking forwards, no longer referencing everything in the past, and these were the seeds of hope.

Then there was another dream. I am with a woman, not a real person or anyone I know, and we are overcoming obstacles and problems together. There is a feeling of love. This has the feeling of the Garden of Eden before the forbidden fruit was bitten. There is a feeling of being allowed to love again. I am being asked to and the offer will be accepted. I am being invited to rejoin the human race. It is a very pleasant feeling with which to wake.

It is good to spend more time looking forward than backward, to spend more time with plans than memories. I was at a Humanist funeral a while back, celebrating a life well lived by a man who left us all too soon. There were photos and music and some well-chosen words. He would have enjoyed it.

That night a few of us were chatting about what sort of send-off we would like. It came to my turn. I knew what I wanted and had even written it in my will. I told the story of something that happened one sunny summer morning when I was on a Bateaux Verts ferry in the Bay of St

111

Tropez, a place I have been visiting for years and one of my favourite places on earth. There were regular passengers plus a large group of family and friends who were clearly together. The captain stopped the boat and took the microphone and explained to us all that he was sure we wouldn't mind delaying for a few minutes for the family to scatter the ashes of their loved one on the sea.

I would like that, I said, happy that I had held the group's attention.

My sister was apoplectic.

But you weren't there. That was us. We told you that story!

There are real memories, constructed memories and some that are downright stolen. Every time we recall them they change a little, and that is one of the foundation stones of therapy.

I ring my mum and dad. My dad answers. They are in bed. That is odd as there never was a bedside phone. I tell him I have to put off seeing them at the weekend. I have an unexpected golf game. No problem, he says. Then I hear her voice as well, as he explains. For the first time I am listening to both of their voices. I had forgotten her accent was quite country.

It never really mattered much what I did or said. They just loved me.

ACKNOWLEDGEMENTS

Firstly, I have to acknowledge Covid 19. There is nothing good to say about this virus but with long hours at home I read Ulysses after many attempts, and wrote this long column.

In January 2021, during a short window when we could see real people, I was presenting a radio show on KCLR96FM. Two of my guests were writers and performers John MacKenna and Angela Keogh. In the course of the conversation they mentioned that they had also become publishers. I googled The Harvest Press when I got home and a week later submitted three sample chapters in Times New Roman as instructed. With their support and guidance I got from there to here.

A small group of trusted friends, and family, read the manuscripts at various stages and made helpful comments, some of which will have found their way into the final text. They include Jennifer McCreery, Dr Fiona Kelly Meldon, John Purcell, and my long time *Sunday Independent* Editor, Mary O'Sullivan. I take responsibility alone for what appears between the covers.